JANE AUSTEN

A Study of Her Artistic Development

JANE AUSTEN

A Study of Her Artistic Development

A. WALTON LITZ

NEW YORK

OXFORD UNIVERSITY PRESS

1965

65—05988

PREFACE

It should not be surprising that the largest claims for Jane Austen's art have been made in our own time. The success of modern criticism in analyzing works of fiction by methods formerly associated with the study of lyric poetry has made the traditional objections to Jane Austen's limited subject-matter seem almost irrelevant. By emphasizing her control of language and mastery of ironic exposure, recent critics have greatly expanded our appreciation of what Jane Austen accomplished on her "little bit (two Inches wide) of Ivory."

Inevitably, this discovery of a new and rewarding approach to Jane Austen's fiction has led to a neglect—and in some instances a rejection—of the characteristics which delighted earlier readers. There has been a tendency to present her as a radical dissenter whose "subversive" aims (subversive to the moral and social orders of her age) have only become apparent in the perspective of modern life. This is, at best, a partial truth; and the present need would seem to be for studies which attempt to connect Jane Austen's critical irony and command of narrative technique with the other qualities of her art. I would agree with Ian Watt that "the criticism of Jane Austen in the last two decades is incomparably the richest and most illuminating that has appeared"; but I am equally in accord with Watt's strictures on this criticism.

> . . . in demonstrating how the restrictions of her subject matter are the basis for a major literary achievement, recent criticism has perhaps failed to give the nature of Jane Austen's social and moral assumptions an equally exacting analysis. It is surely mistaken to assume that the affirmative elements in her morality and her humor are not as real as the subversive ironies which occasionally accompany them; or even to assume that awareness and insight, so often, and rightly, ascribed either to Jane Austen as narrator or to her major characters, are self-sufficient virtues: for how one sees is surely not more important than what one makes a point of seeing, or not seeing.[1]

In the present study I have tried to combine our new understanding of Jane Austen's techniques with an examination of the moral and literary backgrounds of the novels. My emphasis has been on the development of her individual vision, and its relationship to tradition and convention.

The proportions and organization of this study may need some justification. I have nowhere attempted a full-scale "reading" of a single work; instead, I have concentrated upon those aspects of each work which strike me as significant in the context of Jane Austen's artistic development. This focus on her total achievement has demanded a close study of the minor works and fragments, since in some ways they are just as revealing as the masterpieces. When we try to understand Jane Austen's reactions to the literature of her own age the juvenile works take on a special importance, and for this reason I have treated them in some detail. Indeed, the first chapter goes beyond the *Juvenilia* to an examination of the sources of Jane

[1] *Jane Austen: A Collection of Critical Essays,* ed. Ian Watt, Englewood Cliffs, N.J., 1963, p. 13.

Austen's art, and in doing so it lays the groundwork for later discussions. Throughout this study I have had in mind an audience familiar with the major novels and the significant criticism of them, but I have not assumed a familiarity with the minor pieces. Where excellent analyses of a particular work are available (this is especially true of *Emma* and *Pride and Prejudice*) I have not hesitated to direct the reader to them for support of my own argument.

In any study of Jane Austen's artistic development the dating of the works becomes a crucial matter. To a large extent the critic's conclusions are determined by the sequence in which he treats the works. For this reason I have given particular attention to the chronology of composition, but in order to avoid excessive detail in the critical chapters I have relegated the evidence on dating to an Appendix.

I hope my specific debts to other critics are fully acknowledged in the footnotes and text, but some of my obligations go beyond isolated quotations. From Mary Lascelles's *Jane Austen and Her Art*, probably the best general study yet produced, I first learned the importance of viewing the novels against the background of late eighteenth-century literature. Although I am in profound disagreement with Marvin Mudrick's argument in his *Jane Austen: Irony as Defense and Discovery*, I have always profited from this disagreement; Mudrick's emphasis on a unified view of Jane Austen's entire achievement is especially valuable. To Lionel Trilling's brilliant article on *Mansfield Park* [2] I owe more than a new appreciation of that novel; Trilling's general ideas have aided me in my approach to the moral conflicts which underlie all the works. Howard S. Babb's fine study of Jane Austen's skill in dialogue (*Jane Austen's Novels: The Fabric of Dialogue*) did not appear until my own book was nearly completed, but I have been pleased to find confirmation of many of my ideas in his particular

[2] In *The Opposing Self,* New York, 1955, pp. 206–30.

analyses. For an increased understanding of the English novel before Jane Austen I am indebted to Ian Watt's comprehensive study, *The Rise of the Novel*. To Andrew Wright and B. C. Southam I feel a special obligation, not only for the aid of their writings but for stimulating conversations about Jane Austen. Finally, I must acknowledge my gratitude to the late R. W. Chapman, whose scholarship is the foundation of all modern Austen criticism.

This book was begun under a fellowship from the American Council of Learned Societies, and I would like to take this opportunity to express my appreciation for the Council's generous support.

Princeton, New Jersey   A.W.L.
December 1964

DOCUMENTATION

Unless otherwise indicated, all citations of Jane Austen's fiction are based on the edition of R. W. Chapman (5 Vols., 3rd edn., Oxford, 1933; and Vol. VI, *Minor Works*, Oxford, 1954). Page references are inserted directly into the text.

Quotations from *Volume the Second* of the *Juvenilia* are based upon B. C. Southam's authoritative edition of the manuscript (Oxford, 1963), but for ease of reference I have followed the pagination of *Minor Works*.

Abbreviations for the works frequently cited are:

Lascelles   Mary Lascelles, *Jane Austen and Her Art*, London, 1939.

Letters   *Jane Austen's Letters to Her Sister Cassandra and Others*, ed. R. W. Chapman, 2nd edn., Oxford, 1952. Wherever possible I have referred to the dates of the letters.

Life   William and R. A. Austen-Leigh, *Jane Austen, Her Life and Letters, A Family Record*, London, 1913.

Memoir   James Edward Austen-Leigh, *Memoir of Jane Austen*, ed. R. W. Chapman, Oxford, 1926 (first published in 1870).

Mudrick   Marvin Mudrick, *Jane Austen: Irony as Defense and Discovery*, Princeton, 1952.

CONTENTS

JANE AUSTEN

A Study of Her Artistic Development

I

THE LAND OF FICTION

Juvenilia and *Lady Susan*

We call Jane Austen the first "modern" English novelist because she was the first writer of fiction who synthesized the achievements of Fielding and Richardson, thus anticipating the classic form of the nineteenth-century novel, a form that enables the artist to record both the flow of external events and the complexities of personal impressions.[1] In making this synthesis, and in rejecting the late eighteenth-century fashions in fiction, Jane Austen performed an act of criticism that places the history of the eighteenth-century English novel in perspective and foreshadows the course of much nineteenth-century English fiction. Many of the narrative principles formulated by James and Forster are implicit in her mature work, and the fact that she never articulated these principles does not indicate that she was unaware of them. For Jane Austen was a supremely conscious artist, and the best evidence of her awareness lies in her incisive criticism of the fiction of her own age, a criticism found not in letters or prefaces but in the burlesques and parodies of her early career.

3

At the time when Jane Austen first began to examine the literary fashions of her society, in the early 1790's, criticism of the English novel had not advanced beyond that found in the age of Richardson and Fielding. Few writers had followed the example set by Fielding in his Preface to *Joseph Andrews* and the Introductory Chapters of *Tom Jones,* and most criticism of fiction still echoed Dr. Johnson's concern with the moral impact of an art-form that strove to imitate the actual rather than the ideal.[2] The era of serious attention to the art of fiction did not begin until near the end of Jane Austen's lifetime; indeed, Scott's review of *Emma* in the *Quarterly Review* (1815) marks a turning-point in the criticism of the novel.[3] For a young girl living in a small Hampshire village in the last decade of the eighteenth century, the most cogent critiques of the improbable plots and artificial language which characterized contemporary fiction would be found in a few satiric works: Charlotte Lennox's *Female Quixote* (1752), aimed at the romances of an earlier generation; Sheridan's dramas, especially *The Rivals* and *The Critic;* and perhaps George Colman's *Polly Honeycombe* (1760), an early burlesque of sentimental fiction and the circulating libraries. Widespread ridicule of the debased standards in current fiction was yet to come, and it is a sign of Jane Austen's genius—and her familiarity with contemporary fiction—that she should anticipate this reversal in taste.[4] Many readers have been misled by the triviality of much of her correspondence, and by the deceptive simplicity of her novels, into holding the opinion (reminiscent of the neo-classic reaction to Shakespeare) that Jane Austen was a natural genius, an inspired Fanny Burney with a finer ear for conversation and a keener eye for contemporary manners. Yet even a superficial examination of her reading and her early fiction will prove that Jane Austen was an unusually well-read artist who constantly measured her own talents against those of other writers.[5] F. R. Leavis sees in the connections between Jane Austen's reading and her art a perfect example of the "relations of the 'individual talent' to tradition."

> If the influences bearing on her hadn't comprised something fairly to be called tradition she couldn't have found herself and her true direction; but her relation to tradition is a creative one. She not only makes tradition for those coming after, but . . . creates the tradition we see leading down to her. Her work, like the work of all great creative writers, gives a meaning to the past.[6]

Leavis is certainly right in applying to Jane Austen the argument of T. S. Eliot's "Tradition and the Individual Talent." Although in her own lifetime her achievement was vastly overshadowed by that of Scott, and although she cannot be reckoned as a crucial influence on the development of the nineteenth-century English novel, more and more readers are beginning to realize that Jane Austen's works define the important differences between eighteenth-century and nineteenth-century English fiction, illuminating the achievements of both earlier and later novelists.

When the young Jane Austen looked about her in the fiction of the time, she found a rich field in which to exercise her natural gift for critical irony. During the fifty years from 1740 to 1790 the annual production of works of fiction increased from approximately twenty to over eighty, and this accelerated production was matched by a decline in quality.[7] As the reading audience rapidly widened, the influence of the few intelligent commentators waned, and popular taste fell under the control of those readers (mainly women) who patronized the sentimental fiction of the circulating libraries. The average reader, like Sheridan's Lydia Languish, resorted to fiction for emotional titillation, and Sir Anthony Absolute's denunciation of the circulating libraries (". . . a circulating library in a town is as an evergreen tree of diabolical knowledge! It blossoms through the year!") was the comic echo of a serious moral position.[8] In the eighteenth century books were expensive, making the reading public largely dependent upon the circulating libraries for its fictions, and these libraries often catered to the lowest common denominator of taste. Faced with an economic situation that fostered mediocrity, and hampered by the absence of intelligent critics who could assess and direct the new genre, most late eighteenth-century novelists lacked any sense of a vital and evolving tradition. Writers tended to imitate one another; there was a proliferation of minor "schools" of fiction; and within these schools originality was subordinated to conventional situations, stock responses, and a "group" style. By 1790 the typical English novel was almost a parody of itself, and the way lay open for Jane Austen's cleansing irony.

In *The Borough* (1810) Crabbe condemned the average novel's lifeless characters as "creatures borrow'd and again convey'd / From book to book—the shadows of a shade"; and in his review of *Emma* Scott observed that the reader of popular novels gradually "became familiar with the land of fiction, the adventures of which he assimilated not with those of real life, but with each other." [9] These are just observations on English prose fiction at the end of the eighteenth century. The "land of fiction" surveyed by the young Jane Austen was a strange and absurd world, in which the actions of the characters obeyed the "laws" of fiction rather than probability, and the author's point-of-view was determined by literary habit. Such a world was ready-made for the probing criticism of her early style, since burlesque and parody are most effective when directed against the "rules" of life or art. In her *Juvenilia* Jane Austen carried the laws of the "land of fiction" to their logical ends, and then tested the resulting absurdity against her own sense of reality. In so doing she accomplished the double purpose of exposing false literature and false morality while developing her personal style. In the burlesques of the *Juvenilia* she began to explore the stylistic and moral complexities (these reflections of each other) that were to be the subjects of her mature fiction; beneath her criticisms of bad art we find the beginnings of her intricate criticism of life. The best of Jane Austen's nineteenth-century critics, an anonymous contributor to the *North British Review* (1870), was the first to face this issue squarely:

> . . . her parodies were designed not so much to flout at the style as at the unnaturalness, unreality, and fictitious morality, of the romances she imitated. She began by being an ironical critic . . . This critical spirit lies at the foundation of her artistic faculty.[10]

Since the novel, of all art forms, is most dependent on a clear understanding of the circumstances of everyday life, we can view Jane Austen's early attacks on the "fictitious" behavior and morality of the popular novel as preparation for her own scrupulous examination of contemporary manners. And to understand these attacks fully we must know something of the kind of fiction against which they were aimed.

Jane Austen's major target in her *Juvenilia* was the novel of sentiment or sensibility, the dominant form of popular fiction in the late eighteenth century. In general the terms "sentimental novel" and "novel of sensibility" may be used interchangeably (they were so used in the eighteenth century), but for our special purpose we may confine the "novels of sensibility" to those works produced after 1765–70, when the French influence had become pronounced and the excesses of the earlier sentimental fiction had been accepted as the norm.[11] Late in the century Clara Reeve, in the Preface to her *School for Widows*, could look back on a rapid degeneration of the terms "sentimental" and "sensibility":

> This word [sentimental], like many others, seems to have de-
> generated from its original meaning: and, under this flimsy dis-
> guise, it has given rise to a great number of whining, maudlin
> stories, full of false sentiment and false delicacy, calculated to
> excite a kind of morbid sensibility, which is to faint under every
> ideal distress, and every fantastical trial; which have a tendency
> to weaken the mind, and to deprive it of those resources which
> Nature intended it should find within itself.[12]

Clara Reeve's lament over "false sentiment" and "morbid
sensibility" appears less blatantly moralistic when we examine
the philosophic connections of these terms; and an understanding of the philosophic implications is important for an
appreciation of Jane Austen's ambivalent attitude toward "sentiment" and "feeling." Actually, as I shall demonstrate in later
chapters, the notions of "feeling" and "sensibility" current in
the "land of fiction" were gross debasements of the Shaftes-
burian "moral sense," the final corruption of that amiable system of benevolence and right feeling which is one of the major
strains in eighteenth-century thought. It is important to recognize this affinity, for Jane Austen herself (or at least part of
her mind) was on the side of benevolence and feeling, of the
"amiable" virtues, and all her works must be seen against the
background of an eighteenth-century dialectic involving Reason and Feeling, Judgment and Fancy. Her reaction against
the debased expressions of feeling and sensibility derived part
of its force from her attachment to the genuine expression of
these qualities. By education and temperament, Jane Austen
was uniquely suited to dramatize in her art the classic debates
of the century that lay behind her.

When we turn to the fiction that Jane Austen burlesqued,
and seek for its moral center, we do not have far to go: there is
a gross equation between value and the sentimental performance, a direct correlation between the worth of a character and
his ability to *display* emotion. This self-centered morality, if it

can be graced with such a term, was the foundation of the novel of sensibility, and against it Jane Austen directed her most penetrating criticisms. In these novels the physiological connotations of the word "sensibility" are emphasized, and delicacy of emotion can only be proved through trembling, tears, hysteria, madness, or fainting. Physical reactions become an index to virtue, and a nineteenth-century editor of Mackenzie's *Man of Feeling* (1771) was only following the author's intent when he compiled an "Index to the tears shed (chokings, etc., not counted)," which contained such entries as:

Eye wet with a tear	page 127
Tears, face bathed with	" 130
Dropped one tear, no more	" 131
Tears, press-gang could not refrain from	" 136 [13]

When sincerity and personal worth are judged by the quantity of emotion exhibited, and the violence of that emotion, the step into parody and burlesque is a short one. In his *Fool of Quality* (1766-72) Henry Brooke, like so many late eighteenth-century novelists, unconsciously takes this step on every page. Here is the reaction of one of Brooke's characters to the death of his wife:

I then rose, and threw myself along the floor, and my faithful and valiant companions immediately gathered to me; but finding that I would not be removed, they cast themselves around me.

All light was shut out save the glimmering of a taper; and for seven nights and seven days we dwelt in silence, except the solemn interruptions of smothered sobs and wailings.[14]

But the sympathetic tears of men of feeling are not reserved for human tragedies alone; witness Brooke's description of the

last days of a sentimental lion who grieves to death over the
loss of his closest friend, a spaniel.

> For five days he [the lion] thus languished, and gradually de-
> clined, without taking any sustenance, or admitting any com-
> fort; till one morning he was found dead, with his head lovingly
> reclined on the carcase of his little friend. They were both in-
> terred together, and their grave plentifully watered by the tears
> of the keeper and his loudly lamenting family.[15]

Faced with the necessity of producing repeated emotional
outbursts of increasing intensity, and desirous of making his
characters more "susceptible" (and therefore more attractive)
than those of his competitors, the typical late eighteenth-century novelist was driven to the fabrication of more and more
improbable plots, until all contact with natural behavior was
lost in the intricacies of melodrama. By 1790 the setting and
action of the average novel of sensibility were scarcely recognizable as part of the solid world inhabited by its readers. As
we shall see when we come to *Northanger Abbey*, the Gothic
novels of the 1790's, and especially those of the Radcliffean
school, were merely extensions of the novel of sensibility:
their fantastic settings were the logical end to the flight from
reality initiated by the earlier works of sensationalism.

   In the improbability of its language and inhabitants the
"land of fiction" could amply justify Jane Austen's early burlesques, but her most serious criticism was reserved for its
"fictitious morality." The novels of sensibility reflected a gradual cheapening of the eighteenth-century ideals of moderation
and balance, a corruption of the noble concepts of "benevolence" and "feeling." But beyond this they had an appreciable
impact on social behavior: the reaction of the female reading
public to them provides a classic example of life imitating art.
Lady Louisa Stuart, remembering her first reading of *The*

Man of Feeling, recorded her fear that she would not cry enough "to gain the credit of proper sensibility." [16] And in her *Diary* for 1780 Fanny Burney recounts a meeting with a young lady of Bath whose reading of "Hume and Bolingbroke" has turned her into a misanthrope, afflicted with *ennui* and pretending to contemplate suicide:

> "You surprise me more and more," cried I [Fanny Burney]; "is it possible you can so rationally see the disease of a disordered imagination, and yet allow it such power over your mind?"
> "Yes, for it is the only source from which I draw any shadow of felicity. Sometimes when in the country, I give way to my imagination for whole days, and then I forget the world and its cares, and feel some enjoyment of existence."
> "Tell me what is then your notion of felicity? Whither does your castle-building carry you?"
> "Oh, quite out of the world—I know not where, but I am surrounded with sylphs, and I forget everything besides." [17]

Marvin Mudrick has said that Jane Austen's early works cut off "the bourgeois escape," disposing of all "the feverish daydreams . . . in which the middle class—especially its unoccupied women—tries guiltily to deny itself," [18] and the passage from Fanny Burney's *Diary* tends to support him. If such a "disordered imagination" could be produced by the reading of Hume and Bolingbroke, what fantasies might not be engendered by the novel, where there is more danger—in Dr. Johnson's words—that the examples will "take Possession of the Memory by a kind of Violence, and produce effects almost without the Intervention of the Will." [19] Jane Austen's younger brother Henry had this danger in mind when he attacked the excesses of sentimentalism in an undergraduate essay:

> For these very sentimentalists themselves, these worshippers of extravagant refinement must confess that the identical works

whence they draw their favorite theories, exhibit the strongest
proofs of their own fallacy. For though these Heroes and
Heroines of sentimental memory be only imaginary characters,
yet we may fairly presume, they were meant to be probable
ones; and hence too we may conclude, that all who adopt their
opinions will share their fate; that they will be tortured by the
poignant delicacy of their own feelings, and fall the Martyrs to
their own Susceptibility.[20]

Here Henry is pointing forward to the method used by his
sister in her *Juvenilia*, where she exposed the absurdity of
those laws that governed the "land of fiction" by following
them in every detail. The result is a devastating irony which
gains in force when we realize that the "fictitious morality" of
the novels of sensibility was often taken for reality. The following inscription, placed on the tomb of a young lady of
Dorchester, might well serve as an epitaph for all the heroes
and heroines of sensibility:

READER!
If thou hast a Heart fam'd for Tenderness and Pity, Contemplate this Spot. In which are deposited the Remains of a Young
Lady, whose artless Beauty, innocence of Mind, and gentle
Manners, once obtained her the Love and Esteem of all who
knew her, But when Nerves were too delicately spun to bear
the rude Shakes and Jostlings which we meet with in this
transitory World, Nature gave way; She sunk and died a Mar-
tyr to Excessive Sensibility.

It is not difficult to imagine what Jane Austen's reaction
would have been if she had encountered this epitaph: an
ironic smile at the disparity between life and imagination, followed perhaps by a biting reference in a letter to Cassandra.
But one must insist that the irony which Jane Austen brings
to bear on the "land of fiction" is not entirely an aloof and de-

tached commentary on life's incongruities; it is also an attack on the sentimentalist and romantic within herself. For Jane Austen the artist was committed both to a Johnsonian system of morality and a "pre-romantic" feeling for life, and no simple formula can explain the subtleties and contradictions of her fiction. It will not do to say—as Marvin Mudrick does—that her characteristic reaction is a defensive, aloof, unemotional irony, and that this characteristic attitude is occasionally overwhelmed, to the detriment of her art, by the forces of conventional society.[21] *Pride and Prejudice* and *Mansfield Park* are both "characteristic" of their author, and neither alone gives a full sense of her complex vision. Jane Austen does not oscillate between defiance of society and capitulation to its demands; instead, she dramatizes the conflicts within her own personality and environment, conflicts between Reason and Feeling, classic restraint and individual freedom, society and the free spirit. And it is these conflicts, most often cast in eighteenth-century terms, which give life and coherence to all her works.

One measure of the extent to which the late eighteenth century was concerned with the effects of "fictitious morality" upon behavior may be found in the popular "Quixotic" formula for the satiric novel.[22] In the "Quixotic" novel the hero or heroine, having received a false view of the world from literature, embarks on a series of adventures which expose the absurdity of his *idée fixe;* the disparity between idea and reality produces comic-moralistic effects. This conventional plot structure underlies much of the *Juvenilia,* and is used with great skill in the sub-plot of *Northanger Abbey* and the construction of *Emma;* but Jane Austen differs from the other exploiters of the formula in the subtlety of her presiding vision. Like Cervantes or the Flaubert of *Madame Bovary,* she is able in her best work to encompass both sides of the argument, to assess the absurdities of "sense" as well as those of hyper-imaginative "sensibility." Unlike the average manipulator of the "Quixotic" plot, Jane Austen never places the full weight of reality on one side or the other. Because she persistently burlesques the improbabilities of bad sentimental novels, it has been assumed that she was as sensible as her Elinor; because she laughs at the machinery of the Gothic novel, it has been suggested that she and Mrs. Radcliffe represented opposite positions in the fiction of their age. Yet burlesque and parody are not necessarily acts of rejection, and if they are then the rejection is likely to be of something within the writer's own nature. It is well to remember that William Beckford, the creator of *Vathek* and builder of the fantastic Fonthill Abbey, was also the author of a skillful attack on the novel of sensibility (*Modern Novel Writing, or The Elegant Enthusiast*). And in 1791, the year after Jane Austen completed *Love and Freindship*, a sixteen-year-old Oxford undergraduate wrote a fragmentary burlesque of the current novel which makes many of the same criticisms; his name was Matthew Gregory Lewis, and four years later he was to write the most sensational of all Gothic novels, *The Monk*.[23] There was more than a touch of Mrs. Radcliffe in the young Jane Austen, and *Northanger Abbey* is partly self-criticism. We must be careful not to view the early works as blanket rejections of the "amiable virtues," Feeling and Sentiment; rather they should be considered as searching criticisms of the corruptions of Sentiment and Feeling expressed in the art of the time. It cannot be said that Jane Austen's target in her early works was either bad art or bad morality, for she saw the two as functions of each other.

Before we examine the *Juvenilia* in detail one further question should be considered: how did Jane Austen learn the techniques of burlesque and parody? For although the novels she mocks verge on self-parody, and although she was endowed with a keen native sense of irony, the methods of comic exaggeration must still be learned. The question can be answered in part from what we know of her early reading and environment. Sheridan's *Rivals* was acted at Steventon in 1784, followed by a series of humorous theatricals, and her *History of England* and *Love and Freindship* testify that she was familiar with *The Critic* before 1790.[24] At an early age she had read Charlotte Lennox's *Female Quixote*, and must have been acquainted with other burlesques of bad fiction. But more important than any specific reading was the atmosphere of laughter and self-criticism that pervaded the Austen household. For a knowledge of this family habit of ironical criticism we do not have to rely on second-hand biographical accounts, since in 1789–90 Jane's oldest brother, James Austen, then a young don at St. John's College, Oxford, brought out a periodical which reflects the tastes and critical assumptions of the close-knit Austen family. Called *The Loiterer*, this essay-type periodical (modeled on Mackenzie's *Lounger* and Johnson's *Rambler*) ran for sixty issues, of which thirty-seven were written by James Austen or his younger brother, Henry.[25] Since Henry was Jane's "favorite brother," and James is generally credited with playing an important role in the shaping of her literary taste,[26] we may assume that the essays in *The Loiterer* written by James and Henry embody opinions and habits of mind which helped to determine Jane Austen's artistic development. Jane would certainly have read the essays, and may have helped to plan those written during the Oxford vacations. The comic methods used by James and Henry are close to those employed in the *Juvenilia*, and although none of the *Loiterer* essays can be compared with the best of Jane Austen's early fiction, many of them remind us of the "second stage" in her literary development, when she was hovering "between burlesque and immature story-telling." [27] In *The Loiterer*, as in the later *Juvenilia*, straightforward parody and moral commentary are always changing into more complex narrative forms with a high dramatic content.

One illustration from *The Loiterer* will serve to show its affinity with Jane Austen's early subjects and methods. In essay No. 9 James introduces a long letter from a fictitious "Sophia Sentiment" in which the editors of *The Loiterer* are taken to task for ignoring the fashions of current fiction. Sophia identifies herself as a "great reader" who has not only read "some hundred volumes of Novels and Plays," but has "actually got through all the entertaining papers of our most celebrated periodical writers." She adds that she looked forward with great eagerness to the appearance of *The Loiterer,* but found it "the stupidest work of the kind I ever saw."

Only conceive, in eight papers, not one sentimental story about love and honour, and all that.—Not one Eastern Tale full of Bashas and Hermits, Pyramids and Mosques—no, not even an allegory or dream have yet made their appearance in the Loiterer. . . . As for your last paper, indeed, the story was good enough, but there was no love, and no lady in it, at least no young lady; and I wonder how you could be guilty of such an omission, especially when it could have been so easily avoided. Instead of retiring to Yorkshire, he might have fled into France, and there, you know, you might have made him fall in love with a French *Paysanne,* who might have turned out to be some great person. Or you might have let him set fire to a convent, and carry off a nun, whom he might afterwards have converted, or any thing of that kind, just to have created a little bustle, and made the story more interesting. . . . let us see some nice affecting stories, relating the misfortunes of two lovers, who died suddenly, just as they were going to church. Let the lover be killed in a duel, or lost at sea, or you may make him shoot himself, just as you please; and as for his mistress, she will of course go mad; or if you will, you may kill the lady, and let the lover run mad; only remember, whatever you do, that your hero and heroine must possess a great deal of feeling, and have very pretty names.

James's reply to "Sophia Sentiment" is an ironic rejection of "Novels, Eastern Tales, and Dreams." Of novels there are too many, while dreams only prove that sleep is infectious; and as for Eastern Tales, they are no longer novelties, and their moral messages can no longer be ignored.

> For the fine ladies of the present age are much too wise to be entrapt into virtue by such underhand means, and I should fear would turn in disgust from an Eastern Tale, when they know that a Dervise and a Mosque mean, in plain English, a Parson and a Church, two things that have been so long and so justly voted *bores.* . . .

This essay reminds us that current tastes in fiction were frequently the topic of discussion in the Austen household, and that Jane's own burlesques of Gothic conventions and "novel slang" were the product of a critical habit of mind shared with her brothers and perhaps learned from them.

After this brief survey of the objects of Jane Austen's early irony and some of the origins of her comic techniques, it is time to look at the *Juvenilia* in detail. These minor works, collected in three manuscript volumes, were written by Jane Austen between the ages of twelve or so and seventeen; that is, before 1793. They fall into two groups: first, a collection of high-spirited burlesques culminating in *Love and Freindship* (these include *The History of England* and most of the pieces in *Volume the First*); second, a series of ambiguous pieces in which Jane Austen was moving from burlesque toward more complex narrative forms, and in which we see the world of the major novels taking shape. The writing of these *Juvenilia* was followed (probably in 1794 or 1795) by the composition of *Lady Susan*, which stands squarely between the adolescent and mature works. In considering these early productions we must bear in mind that they are chiefly important in relation to the major novels, and that an assessment of their place in Jane Austen's artistic career should take precedence over any search for "sources." Although many of the *Juvenilia* were written with specific contemporary works in mind, I have tried to avoid wherever possible the byways of literary detection. The *Juvenilia* are remarkably self-sufficient, and most of the burlesque passages are self-explanatory. As Mary Lascelles points out,

> From *Volume the First* onward [Jane Austen] very seldom aims merely at this or that wretched novel or novelist. It is her way to strike through a particular novel, or type of novel, to the false conventions that govern it, and through these conventions to the false taste (in writer and reader alike) that have allowed them to come into being.[28]

The sameness of style and situation which marks most late eighteenth-century fiction makes it extremely hazardous to claim one work as the major source for any of the *Juvenilia*. For example, C. L. Thomson has suggested that the climax of Mackenzie's *Man of Feeling*, where the hero and heroine collapse together, may have inspired that scene in *Love and Freindship* where Laura and Sophia, overcome by the emotional meeting with their husbands, faint "Alternately on a Sofa" (86).[29] But it is much more likely that Jane Austen had Sheridan's *The Critic* in mind, for in the under-plot of Puff's play, after the burlesque recognition scene in which the Justice and his Lady "discover" their long-lost son, we find the stage direction: *"They faint alternately in each other's arms."* [30] Wherever I have made references to contemporary works in my discussion of the *Juvenilia* it has been either because the literary relationship is illuminating, or because we have definite evidence that Jane Austen knew a particular work.

One of the most remarkable things about *Love and Freindship* is the date appended to the manuscript: "Finis June 13th

1790." This date not only reveals Jane Austen's precocious talent (she was then less than fifteen) but also her sensitivity to current literary fashions. In 1790 the novel of sensibility had reached its greatest popularity as well as its greatest absurdity, and the moment for reaction had come. In the next decade the number of attacks and burlesques would rapidly increase.[31] Jane Austen's first major assault on the form coincided exactly with this turn in popular feeling, just as nine years later *Northanger Abbey* (in its earliest version) would coincide with the beginnings of a popular reaction against the Gothic novel. Such timing attests to her familiarity with the literary scene as well as to her artistic shrewdness, and makes it possible for us to view *Love and Freindship* and *Northanger Abbey* as definitive comments on the history of late eighteenth-century fiction.

It would be almost impossible to summarize the action of *Love and Freindship*, since one of Jane Austen's aims was to satirize the intricate and unnatural plots of contemporary fiction by making her own plot even more complex and confusing. *Love and Freindship* is a compendium of all the stock situations and stock responses of the novel of sensibility: exotic parentage, revolt against authority, fantastic recognition scenes, love-at-first-sight, a propensity for self-revelation. But throughout it all Jane Austen manages to maintain a clear awareness of the *normal* as well as the *literary* reaction to each situation, so that we have a double sense of the characters in relation to the laws of the "land of fiction" and in relation to the standards of probable social behavior. By applying the rules of the "land of fiction" with rigorous logic Jane Austen exposes the essential unreality of popular novels. In Meredith's *Ordeal of Richard Feverel* Sir Austin defines sentimentality as the desire to enjoy reality "without incurring the Immense Debtorship for a thing done," and it is Jane Austen's purpose to show that the novel of sensibility is founded on this dishonest emotion.

The contempt for material wealth so characteristic of the novel of sensibility is carried to its logical end in *Love and Freindship*: dishonesty of emotion becomes dishonesty of action, and Augustus is praised for purloining money "from his Unworthy father's Escritoire" (88), just as Sophia's theft from Macdonald is justified by his lack of sensibility (96). Since display of emotion is the only index to value, all other standards are jettisoned. Jane Austen shows that the final corruption of the individual "moral sense" is selfishness, and she demonstrates that false sensibility is founded upon self-interest. Augustus and Sophia reject all human intercourse in the name of Excessive Sensibility: ". . . as their Happiness centered wholly in themselves, they wished for no other society" (87).

Among those conventions which Jane Austen burlesques is the equation of fainting with delicate sensibility. Laura and Sophia collapse at every crisis in the action; when they discover Edward and Augustus "weltering" in blood they are deprived of their senses for over an hour, Sophia fainting every moment and Laura running mad (99). When Edward dies Laura gives way to a dramatic delirium reminiscent of the heroine's hysteria in Fanny Burney's *Cecilia*:

> "Talk not to me of Phaetons (said I, raving in a frantic, incoherent manner)—Give me a violin—. I'll play to him & sooth him in his melancholy Hours—Beware ye gentle Nymphs of Cupid's Thunderbolts, avoid the piercing Shafts of Jupiter—Look at that Grove of Firs—I see a Leg of Mutton—They told me Edward was not Dead; but they deceived me—they took him for a Cucumber—" (100)

If this burlesque seems overdone, we must remember that the "set" scenes in the serious fiction of the time were almost as absurd. In Elizabeth Nugent Bromley's *Laura and Augustus* (1784), Laura is "in successive fits" for six hours after the death of Augustus, and she awakens only to run mad.[32] What distinguishes Jane Austen's brilliant burlesque from the novels of sensibility she attacks is not her consistent exaggeration, for it would be hard to exaggerate the absurdities of some of these works, but rather her exposure of the selfish foundation to sensibility. Sophia's last words emphasize this egotism:

> ". . . beware of fainting-fits . . . Though at the time they may be refreshing & Agreable yet beleive me they will in the end, if too often repeated & at improper seasons, prove destructive to your Constitution . . . My fate will teach you this . . . I die a Martyr to my greif for the loss of Augustus. . . . One fatal swoon has cost me my Life. . . . Beware of swoons Dear Laura . . . A frenzy fit is not one quarter so pernicious; it is an exercise to the Body & if not too violent, is I dare say conducive to Health in its consequences—Run mad as often as you chuse; but do not faint—" (102)

Typical of Jane Austen's deflationary method in *Love and Freindship* is the episode satirizing the convention of "recognition," where four grandchildren are revealed in as many minutes (91–2). Here she must have had in mind that scene from Sheridan's *The Critic* where the Justice acknowledges his long-lost son:

> No Orphan, nor without a Friend art thou—
> I am thy Father; here's thy Mother; there
> Thy uncle—this thy first cousin, and Those
> Are all your near Relations! (III,i)

So far Jane Austen's technique of extravagant exaggeration corresponds with that of Sheridan; but the recognition scene in *Love and Freindship* ends on an entirely different note. Instead of being overcome by emotion, as is the Justice, Laura's grandfather looks "fearfully towards the Door" (92) and inquires: "tell me, have I any other Grand-Children in the House."

"None my Lord." "Then I will provide for you all without further delay—Here are 4 Banknotes of 50£ each—Take them &
remember I have done the Duty of a Grandfather—." He instantly left the Room & immediately afterwards the House.
(92)

Already we can see Jane Austen, discontented with the limited black-and-white judgments of burlesque, striving toward
a more complex comedy.

Some parts of *Love and Freindship* are straightforward burlesque; typical of these is the reaction of Laura and Sophia to
the young Man chosen for Janetta.

They said he was Sensible, well-informed, and Agreable; we
did not pretend to Judge of such trifles, but as we were convinced he had no soul, that he had never read the Sorrows of
Werter, & that his Hair bore not the slightest resemblance to
Auburn, we were certain that Janetta could feel no affection for
him, or at least that she ought to feel none. (93)

This straightforward lampoon already seems a bit out of place,
a bit crude, in the total context of *Love and Freindship*, but
it is characteristic of the short burlesques in *Volume the First*,
and for this reason I would assume that most of the humorous
fragments in *Volume the First* originated before 1790, even if
their dedications (and fair copies) date from a slightly later
period. Taken together they form a catalogue of the incongruities in the novel of sensibility that amused the young Jane
Austen; in them the satire is broader, the objects of burlesque
more purely literary than in *Love and Freindship*. The targets
range from fawning Dedications ("The Beautifull Cassandra")
to the hurried tidying-up of the plot at the end of a conventional drama ("The Visit"), from hackneyed pastoral machinery ("Frederic & Elfrida") to the inevitably flawless hero
(Charles Adams, in "Jack & Alice," who had "so dazzling a

Beauty that none but Eagles could look him in the Face"). In "Amelia Webster" Jane Austen pokes fun at the inevitability of love-at-first-sight:

> I saw you lovely Fair one as you passed on Monday last, before our House in your way to Bath. I saw you thro' a telescope, & was so struck by your Charms that from that time to this I have not tasted human food. (49)

Mysterious parentage is the subject of ridicule in "Henry & Eliza." Nor are those twin indexes of sensibility, tears and fainting, ever neglected. In "Frederic & Elfrida" the heroine is so distressed that she has "scarcely patience enough to recover from one" fainting fit before falling into another (11), while the fair Emma (of "Edgar & Emma") retires to her own room at the end of the tale and continues in tears "the remainder of her Life."

Closer to *Love and Freindship* is the short piece in *Volume the First* that bears the weighty title, "A Beautiful Description of the Different Effects of Sensibility on Different Minds," itself a parody of many sententious eighteenth-century titles. In this *jeu d'esprit* the "insensitive" doctor reduces all of Melissa's self-pitying complaints to dreadful puns.

> "I am come to see Melissa," said he. "How is She?" "Very weak indeed, said the fainting Melissa. "Very weak, replied the punning Doctor, aye indeed it is more than a very *week* since you have taken to your bed . . ." (72)

But the nearest approach to *Love and Freindship* among the short burlesque pieces is the fifth letter in "A Collection of Letters" (*Volume the Second*), where the mockery of love-conventions is handled with a dexterity and maturity of dialogue which suggest the later *Juvenilia*. Here, in contrast with the other burlesques, the language and actions are just within the border of believable human conduct, and Henrietta Halton, with her shabby tastes based on bad fiction, is just such a "female Quixote" as might have existed at the end of the eighteenth century.

When we move from the burlesques to those *Juvenilia* where a serious concern for manners is dominant, we are entering a world alive with suggestions of the later fiction. Here the germs of many later works are to be found in a curious mixture of shrewd original observations and stock situations borrowed from Richardson or Fanny Burney. Many of the names used in the major novels are present, and the situations are suggestive of later plots.[33] But it would be a mistake to place too much emphasis on the relationships between these fictions and the later novels. The fact is that Jane Austen's world was extremely limited, at least as far as subject-matter was concerned, and once she had sighted the basic situations and personalities of that world there was little room for variation in the details of action and setting. The materials of her art, "3 or 4 Families in a Country Village," [34] were to remain the same, limited scrupulously to that segment of English life which she knew at first hand: development lay in a refinement of the manner in which these situations were treated, and in a deepening of the author's psychological insight. Courtship and marriage were always Jane Austen's concerns, but in her major works she was able to give these commonplace subjects such a range of implication that they figure forth basic conflicts between social-economic necessities and the need for spiritual freedom. In the early burlesques characters representing opposing views of life are pitted against each other; but in the more mature pieces we find a growing tendency to dramatize the opposing forces working within a single personality. Even at the age of fifteen or sixteen Jane Austen felt the need for liberation from the narrow confines of burlesque and parody;

she began to seek for forms in which her maturing vision of reality could be more subtly and consistently expanded.

In "The Three Sisters" (*Volume the First*) Jane Austen explores motives of economic and social aggression which appear in all her mature fictions. Told in the form of letters from two of the sisters, the piece begins with Mary Stanhope's correspondence concerning her impending engagement; then, with the situation established, we move outside Mary's petty mind and see her ensuing actions through the ironic eyes of her lively sister Georgiana. In this short fiction Jane Austen introduces us to the economic and social facts of marriage: here is Mary Stanhope's judgment of her suitor.

> He is quite an old Man, about two & thirty, very plain, so plain that I cannot bear to look at him. He is extremely disagreable & I hate him more than any body else in the world. He has a large fortune & will make great Settlements on me; but then he is very healthy. In short I do not know what to do. If I refuse him he as good as told me that he should offer himself to Sophia and if *she* refused him to Georgiana, & I could not bear to have either of them married before me. (58)

After Mary has exposed her avarice and jealousy in two letters to her friend, Georgiana is allowed to comment on the remainder of the action. She describes Mary's anxious inquiries as to whether the other sisters would accept his offers; recounts the exorbitant and insulting demands; and finally describes the scene where Mary unconsciously reveals her true nature to a handsome stranger, Mr. Brudenell, whose "only Aim was to laugh at her" (69). Throughout her letters Georgiana maintains an aloof and ironic attitude toward her sister's folly; like so many later narrators in Jane Austen's fiction, she stands both within and without the story's action.

One of the most interesting things about "The Three Sisters" is the manner in which it hovers between burlesque and a more subtle comic form. At several points Jane Austen cannot resist pushing the description or dialogue to the burlesque extreme, but in almost every case these incongruous, though amusing, passages have been erased. In writing the following description of Mary's ridiculous demands Jane Austen quite obviously could not resist the temptation to exaggerate; but later, once the tone of the whole piece was established, the words I have italicized were excised, thus restoring the speech to the realm of probability.

> "And Remember I am to have a new Carriage hung as high as the Duttons', & blue spotted with silver; and I shall expect a new saddle horse, a suit of fine lace, and an infinite number of the most valuable Jewels. Diamonds such as never were seen, *Pearls as large as those of the Princess Badroulbadour in the 4th Volume of the Arabian Nights and Rubies, Emeralds, Toppazes, Sapphires, Amythists, Turkeystones, Agate, Beads, Bugles & Garnets* and Pearls, Rubies, Emeralds and Beads out of number." (65)

Again, near the end of "The Three Sisters," when the handsome stranger is introduced as "Sir Henry Brudenell of Leicestershire," Jane Austen at first added the comment:

> Not related to the Family & . . . even but distantly connected with it. His Sister is married to John Dutton's Wife's Brother. When you have puzzled over this account a little you will understand it. (67–8)

But this passage could not stand up to the critical scrutiny of the author, and was ultimately erased.

"Lesley Castle" (*Volume the Second*) is Jane Austen's first attempt to create a variety of believable characters, and to place them in a wholly realistic social milieu; therefore we should not be surprised if the narrative breaks over occasion-

ally into pure burlesque, or subsides into conventional commentary. Although it is the least successful of the long
Juvenilia "Lesley Castle" does represent a distinct advance
over *Love and Freindship,* which was probably written two
years earlier.[35] In Charlotte Lutterell, with her invincible
common-sense and propensity for seeing all of life in household terms, Jane Austen created her first major proponent of
"sense," a full character against whom the representative of
"sensibility" seems pale and insignificant. One wonders if the
contrast between Elinor and Marianne, in the original version
of *Sense and Sensibility,* was equally as broad. Since Charlotte's whole life is dominated by her passion for domestic activities (a passion so inclusive that it prevents all thought of
marriage), she makes an ideal commentator on the activities
of the Lesley family; and her letters to Miss Lesley, heavily
freighted with characteristic similes ("as White as a Whipt
syllabub," "as cool as a cream-cheese") are the life-line of the
story. Marvin Mudrick is right in calling Charlotte "Jane Austen's first independently achieved character"; [36] whereas one
can find prototypes for the other characters in Richardson or
Fanny Burney, Charlotte is entirely of Jane Austen's creation.

"Lesley Castle" is, in some ways, an earlier version of *Lady
Susan.* Susan Lesley and Susan Vernon share similar personalities as well as the same name, and the letter in which Susan
Lesley describes her first reactions to Lesley Castle and her
step-daughters is reminiscent of Susan Vernon's letters from
Churchill to Mrs. Johnson. Lady Lesley lacks the steady assurance and overwhelming sophistication of Lady Susan
Vernon, nor does she have the ability (Lady Susan's great
strength) of complete self-knowledge. But she is more than
the conventional image of a predatory woman-of-fashion, and
one would guess that behind her creation there lay some actual
experience that was also the germ of *Lady Susan.*[37]

In "Lesley Castle," as in "The Three Sisters," the impulse

to parody occasionally intrudes itself. In the first letter, when Margaret Lesley paints a romantic picture of her isolation from the world, Jane Austen cannot resist an ironic comment in the style of *Love and Freindship*:

> But tho' retired from almost all the World, (for we visit no one but the M'Leods, The M'Kenzies, the M'Phersons, the M'Cartneys, the M'donalds, The M'Kinnons, the M'lellans, the M'Kays, the Macbeths and the Macduffs) we are neither dull nor unhappy . . . (111)

The first letter is balanced between burlesque and direct exposition, but from the second letter on there is increasing emphasis on a realistic analysis of manners. However, Jane Austen never seems quite at home in the mode, and the final letter reverts to the world of *Love and Freindship*:

> Matilda had a letter this Morning from Lesley, by which we have the pleasure of finding he is at Naples has turned Roman-catholic, obtained one of the Pope's Bulls for annulling his 1st Marriage and has since actually married a Neapolitan Lady of great Rank & Fortune. He tells us moreover that much the same sort of affair has befallen his first wife the worthless Louisa who is likewise at Naples has turned Roman-catholic, and is soon to be married to a Neapolitan Nobleman of great & Distinguished Merit. (138)

The same mixed tone found in "The Three Sisters" and "Lesley Castle" marks "A Collection of Letters" (*Volume the Second*). The dedication is a parody of elegant alliteration, some of the letters are burlesques, and the entire collection may be a take-off on Richardson's *Familiar Letters*.[38] On the other hand, some of the letters (especially the Third and Fourth) are as mature in conception and execution as anything in the *Juvenilia*. Letter the Third, "From a Young Lady in distressed Circumstances to her friend," probes the relationship between a sensitive young lady of no means and a domineering, brutal aristocrat, and in doing so establishes a pattern of behavior later found in *Pride and Prejudice* (Elizabeth and Lady Catherine de Bourgh). Even at this early age Jane Austen was acutely aware of the alliance between economic and social power, and in Lady Greville she creates an aristocrat of intolerable rudeness and condescension. Lady Greville uses Maria as a foil to herself and her daughters, and takes great delight in public exposure of the "distressed" young lady.

> "Pray Miss Maria in what way of business was your Grandfather? for Miss Mason & I cannot agree whether he was a Grocer or a Bookbinder." I saw that she wanted to mortify me and was resolved if I possibly could to prevent her seeing that her scheme succeeded. "Neither Madam; he was a Wine Merchant." "Aye, I knew he was in some such low way—He broke did not he?" "I beleive not Ma'am." "Did not he abscond?" "I never heard that he did." "At least he died insolvent?" "I was never told so before." "Why was not your Father as poor as a Rat?" "I fancy not;" "Was not he in the Kings Bench once?" "I never saw him there." *She* gave me *such* a look, & turned away in a great passion . . . (158–9)

Here we have an unshaded dramatization of a situation that recurs throughout the novels, although the vulgarity of wealth is never again examined in such extreme form. It is as if Jane Austen, in this piece and in many of the *Juvenilia*, was examining the limits of believable human behavior, painting in broad strokes those social relationships which would be treated with such minute discrimination in her more mature fiction.

Letter the Fourth treats in realistic fashion a situation which might have provided the materials for parody. The Young Lady is introduced to a "very agreable looking Girl named Miss Grenville," and immediately proceeds to "quiz" her in the manner of the sentimental heroine, hoping to establish in a few minutes an air of confession and absolute friendship. Miss Grenville's replies, which are accompanied by sighs and looks of sadness, spur the inquisitive Young Lady on, until finally she makes an offer of "Confidence and Freindship." This is gently yet firmly refused, but, nothing daunted, and with her curiosity aroused, the Young Lady continues her catechism.

> "Do you intend staying long in this part of England Miss Grenville?"
> "Yes Ma'am, some time I beleive."
> "But how will Mr & Mrs Grenville bear your Absence?"
> "They are neither of them alive Ma'am."
> This was an answer I did not expect—I was quite silenced & never felt so awkward in my Life—. (162)

The climax of this letter is shocking to the reader as well as to the importunate Young Lady, and the impact is a product of the realistic social situation Jane Austen has so skillfully established. When in *Love and Freindship* Laura refers to the death of both her parents as a "trifling Circumstance" (89) Jane Austen implies a scathing criticism of the cult of sensibility, but we are untouched by the facts of the situation, for Laura's parents have never been more than fictions; similarly, when Edward and Augustus are found "weltering in their blood" (99) our reaction is laughter—the blood is merely red paint, to be wiped away when the curtain is rung down. But the death of Miss Grenville's parents is presented realistically; her grief is like our own, and her embarrassment is one we feel. The meddling Young Lady resides in the midlands of England, not in the "land of fiction." Here we see Jane Austen moving toward a more profound—and potentially tragic—treatment of illusion and reality.

Although some of the pieces in *Volume the First* and *Volume the Second* bear dates later than those found in *Volume the Third* (6 May 1792 and August 1792), there is no reason to suppose that these are the dates of origin, and we may confidently follow the evidence (both stylistic and circumstantial)[39] which points to the contents of *Volume the Third*— *Evelyn*, and *Catharine or The Bower*—as the most mature of the *Juvenilia*. The first of these pieces, *Evelyn*, is more complicated than would appear on first reading. Although it displays many affinities with the earlier parodies and burlesques, there is a substantial difference in tone between *Evelyn* and, say, *Love and Freindship*. The later work is more concentrated, more focused, in a way more serious; and the criticisms of literary conventions are more obviously criticisms of a moral attitude. Marvin Mudrick speaks of *Evelyn* as "curiously mixed," suffering "from stretches of inappropriate serious narrative," and since the story does not fit his formula for Jane Austen's development he dismisses it as an uneven piece which, after several false starts, finally justifies itself "with a final purely parodic flourish of the sentimental virtues; particularly, beauty, generosity, and love."[40] But such a conclusion underrates the tale and its position in Jane Austen's early view of the world. For *Evelyn* represents a distinct advance over *Love and Freindship*, and helps us to understand Jane Austen's attitude toward the "amiable" virtues of Benevolence and Sympathy.

Evelyn is a small village in Sussex whose inhabitants are completely "amiable," and where life is an imitation—or a mockery—of the golden age. Into this stronghold of generosity comes Mr. Gower, and upon learning that Evelyn is a place untouched by "Misery, Illhealth, or Vice" and inhabited by people of unparalleled "Generosity" and "Greatness of mind," he is eager to settle there. The landlady of the Alehouse directs him to a family, "who tho' warmly attached to the spot, yet from a peculiar Generosity of Disposition would perhaps be willing to oblige you with their house" (181). Arriving at the home of this family, Mr. Gower is struck by the pictur- esque situation of the house, and the Benevolence of its in- habitants, the Webbs. They immediately provide him with a lavish meal, make him a present of one hundred pounds and their "house & Grounds," and bestow their eldest daughter on him, protesting all the while at his Goodness in accepting their Generosity.

For some months Mr. Gower is completely happy, his every wish satisfied, until one day the sight of a rose-blossom reminds him of the original mission which led him to Evelyn, an at- tempt to please his sister Rosa and "soften her affliction" by obtaining "a picture of her unfortunate Lover" who had per- ished on a voyage to the Isle of Wight. This voyage had been arranged by the young man's parents, who disapproved of his marriage to Rosa. It is now four months since Mr. Gower began his quest for the picture; and reminded of his sister by the lovely rose, he writes to assure her that his mission will soon be fulfilled. But instead of a reply from Rosa he receives a note from his family saying that she has died, hastened to her grave by Mr. Gower's "long absence and continued Si- lence." This letter is a great shock to Mr. Gower, so great that in spite of Evelyn's salubrious climate he is afflicted with a fit of the gout; but as soon as he has recovered from this he bids good-by to the "amiable Maria" and sets out to the Castle owned by the family of Rosa's dead lover. There he informs the family of Rosa's death ("That luckless Girl is now no more"), berates them for their lack of sensibility, and de- mands a posthumous consent to the marriage. The family are astonished at this request, and after a few more bitter words Mr. Gower leaves the Gothic castle and returns to Evelyn, where he finds all the servants at tea in his wife's dressing- room:

Surprized at so very unusual a sight, he fainted, on his recovery he found himself on the Sofa, with his wife's maid kneeling by him, chafing his temples with Hungary water—. From her he learned that his beloved Maria had been so much grieved at his departure that she died of a broken heart about 3 hours after his departure. (189)

After arranging for his wife's funeral Mr. Gower returns home "in high health & spirits," only to find his sister Rosa alive; she faints, but revives almost immediately and introduces her brother to her husband, a Mr. Davenport. Mr. Gower is astonished:

But my dearest Rosa said the astonished Gower, I thought you were dead & buried. Why my dr Frederick replied Rosa I wished you to think so, hoping that you would spread the report about the country & it would thus by some means reach— Castle—By this I hoped some how or other to touch the hearts of its inhabitants. It was not till the day before yesterday that I heard of the death of my beloved Henry which I learned from Mr D—who concluded by offering me his hand. I accepted it with transport, & was married yesterday— (190)

Mr. Gower, delighted at his sister's match, soon finds in his home town of Carlisle the landlady he first met in Evelyn, and he instantly makes her an offer of his "hand & heart." She accepts; they are immediately married and return to Evelyn. Only then does he recollect that he has failed to inform Mr. and Mrs. Webb of their daughter's death and his remarriage. He does so, and receives the following reply:

GENEROUS, BEST OF MEN
    how truly we rejoice to hear of your present welfare & happiness! & how truly grateful are we for your unexampled generosity in writing to condole with us on the late unlucky acci-

dent which befel our Maria—I have enclosed a draught on our banker for 30 pounds, which Mr Webb joins with me in entreating you & the aimiable Sarah to accept— (191)

Throughout *Evelyn* there is a general burlesque of the stock situations of the novel of sensibility which reminds one of *Love and Freindship*. Love-at-first-sight, inexplicable lapses of memory, cruel parents, tears and fainting—all come in for their share of the satire. There are also some ironic hits at Gothic atmosphere and scenery, showing that Jane Austen was well aware of the increasing popularity of that form. But the bulk of her irony is reserved for emotional and irrational generosity, Benevolence uncontrolled by Judgment. The ridiculous generosity of Mr. and Mrs. Webb is a parody of the indiscriminate Benevolence so often displayed in the novel of sensibility, as in the following scene from Brooke's *Fool of Quality*:

> . . . Harry took him aside, and having cautioned him in a whisper not to take any notice of what should pass, he stole a bill for one hundred and sixty pounds into his hand, saying softly—It is good first to be honest, so there is what I owe you. And here also is a small matter for your daughter; I did not know till now that we had such a sweet little charge in our family. So saying, he slipped to him another bill of fifty pounds, and then, turning from him, stepped carelessly to his seat, as though nothing had happened.[41]

Another classic example of fictional Generosity and Benevolence in the late eighteenth century may be found in Sarah Scott's *The History of Sir George Ellison* (1766), where the hero, on discovering that his sweetheart loves another but cannot marry him for want of money, gives her two thousand pounds and a trousseau, after which he returns with renewed fervor to his charitable works.

What separates *Evelyn* from the earlier burlesques in the

Juvenilia is Jane Austen's concentration on one aspect of the cult of sensibility, a concentration so intense and so steadily maintained that we must search for the reasons behind it. Whereas in *Love and Freindship* she burlesques the entire range of sentimental techniques, and so adroitly that one could almost reconstruct the typical novel of sensibility from her satire, in *Evelyn* her interest is focused on a single subject: the words "Generosity" and "Benevolence" run through the piece like a litany. And this is because Jane Austen saw in the ridiculous and unrealistic generosity of the sentimental heroes and heroines a grotesque distortion of something to which she was profoundly attracted, that true Benevolence which springs from a natural "moral sense" and the exercise of the "Sympathetic Imagination." [12] Early in *Evelyn* the landlady confesses to Mr. Gower that she has a "simpathetic Soul" (180), and the entire work is a burlesque of the "simpathetic Soul" run riot, unrestrained by Reason or Judgment. The performances of Sir Charles Grandison and his fictional imitators were sentimental exaggerations of those generous actions which, according to Adam Smith, should be produced by an innate "moral sense"; [43] and John Wesley revealed a shrewd recognition of this relationship between sentiment and enthusiastic virtue in his decision to issue an abridged version of Brooke's *Fool of Quality,* a book designed "to promote the religion of the heart." [44] In *Evelyn* Jane Austen strikes out so devastatingly at the literary corruptions of the "religion of the heart" because that religion was one of the poles of her own personality and art. In its comic attack on the abuses of the "Sympathetic Imagination," the faculty which enables us to place ourselves in the position of others and feel for them, *Evelyn* is a forerunner of *Northanger Abbey* and *Sense and Sensibility,* works in which Jane Austen explores the limits of the imagination while affirming its essential role in all moral judgments.

One of the most interesting things in *Evelyn* is the almost allegorical use of an imaginary village in which "neither Misery, Illhealth, or Vice" occurs. This overtly symbolic use of place was a device to which Jane Austen would return, with far greater subtlety, in her last work, the unfinished *Sanditon*. And we find a less striking use of the method in the other story of *Volume the Third, Catharine or The Bower,* where the Bower itself represents qualities of the heroine's personality. Although Jane Austen makes dramatic use of place and setting throughout her major works (witness Mansfield Park itself, or the seasonal cycles in *Emma* and *Persuasion*) it is only in *Volume the Third* and *Sanditon* that she appeals consistently and openly to our sense of place or atmosphere, thus revealing her latent affinities with the "landscape" fiction of Mrs. Radcliffe and her intuitive grasp of the artistic effects that could be achieved by turning "place" into "character."

In *Catharine* the heroine's "shady Bower, the work of her own infantine Labours assisted by those of two young Companions," is a symbolic retreat whose artistic function lies halfway between Pamela's closet and Rappaccini's garden. It is an emblem of her individuality and her social isolation, a symbol of those values which her aunt despises, and a reminder of Catharine's persistent retreats into the illusionary world of daydreams and romantic fiction. It has reminded one critic, David Paul, of Henry James's unobtrusive use of symbolic location, and Paul may be right in emphasizing the Bower's sexual significance.

> . . . the symbolic meaning of the bower is sufficiently clear and concentrated, even if it is not all conscious. It becomes the magnetic centre of the story because it is the Virgin's Bower, the symbol of Catharine's sense of her sexual maturity, of her wish for independence, for secrecy even, from her intrusive aunt. The aunt's determination to have it pulled down exposes the

fact that her wish to protect her niece's virtue is in reality a destructive impulse.[45]

Catharine is Jane Austen's first full-scale attempt to place a heroine in a completely realistic social situation and probe her reactions to the complex (and often contradictory) demands of conventional morality and social custom. Like her namesake in *Northanger Abbey*, Catharine is an inexperienced young girl of natural sensibility whose tastes and attitudes have been shaped in large measure by her reading (the scene in which Catharine quizzes Camilla Stanley on her tastes in literature was rewritten into the famous scene on "horrid" fiction in *Northanger Abbey*), and she considers "warmth of heart" the "highest recommendation in any one" (238). After a sheltered education under the jealous care of her aunt, Mrs. Percival, Catharine is slowly awakening to a sense of her own identity and the world's demands upon her. On the one side she is restricted by the mania for order and propriety displayed by her aunt, who has an almost pathological fear of men and their possible effects on her niece's virtue. Mrs. Percival is the first hypochondriac in Jane Austen's fiction, and here—as in future works—the hypochondria is used as an emblem for fear of reality. Already separated from her aunt's narrow moralistic position by her own warm nature, Catharine is faced on the other side by the temptations of the world beyond her immediate experience, represented by the Stanleys. Although it is hard to believe that Catharine would have long admired the foppish Edward Stanley (this may have been one reason for the story's remaining unfinished), he bursts into her narrow world in fulfillment of her daydreams and temporarily overcomes all her scruples. Edward's romantic entrance into Catharine's emotionally impoverished life, "as handsome as a Prince," is the first example of the Cinderella motif which runs through all of Jane Austen's fiction, both ironically (as in *Sense and*

Sensibility) and directly (as in *Mansfield Park*). Caught up in the fairy-tale, Catharine goes to the dance with Edward and thereby violates Mrs. Percival's sense of decorum; and when Edward's mischievous attempts to increase Mrs. Percival's fears culminate in the passionate scene at the Arbor, Catharine receives this denunciation from her aunt:

"Well; *this* is beyond anything I could have supposed. *Profligate* as I *knew* you to be, I was not prepared for such a sight. This is beyond any thing you ever did *before*; beyond any thing I ever heard of in my Life! Such Impudence, I never witnessed before in such a Girl! And this is the reward for all the cares I have taken in your Education; for all my troubles & Anxieties; and Heaven knows how many they have been! All I wished for, was to breed you up virtuously; I never wanted you to play upon the Harpsichord, or draw better than any one else; but I had hoped to see you respectable and good; to see you able & willing to give an example of Modesty and Virtue to the Young people here abouts. I bought you Blair's Sermons, and Coelebs in Search of a Wife, I gave you the key to my own Library, and borrowed a great many good books of my Neighbours for you, all to this purpose. But I might have spared myself the trouble—Oh! Catherine, you are an abandoned Creature, and I do not know what will become of you. I am glad however, she continued softening into some degree of Mildness, to see that you have some shame for what you have done, and if you are really sorry for it, and your future life is a life of penitence and reformation perhaps you may be forgiven. But I plainly see that every thing is going to sixes & sevens and all order will soon be at an end throughout the Kingdom."

"Not however Ma'am the sooner, I hope, from any conduct of mine, said Catherine in a tone of great humility, for upon my honour I have done nothing this evening that can contribute to overthrow the establishment of the kingdom."

"You are Mistaken Child, replied she; the welfare of every Nation depends upon the virtue of it's individuals, and any one who offends in so gross a manner against decorum & propriety is certainly hastening it's ruin. You have been giving a bad example to the World, and the World is but too well disposed to receive such." (232–3)

Such rigid and imperceptive moralizing, based on a neurotic misunderstanding of Catharine's nature and actions, can only drive Catharine farther from "sense" and closer to "sensibility," and the fragment nears conclusion with a symbolic statement of the changes wrought in Catharine's adolescent world: "Her bower alone retained its interest in her feelings, & perhaps that was oweing to the particular remembrance it brought to her mind of Ed^wd Stanley." (239).

Catharine ends with the heroine's original illusions shattered, and there is little doubt that—if Jane Austen had continued the story—the next stage in Catharine's development would have been the destruction of the illusions fostered by Stanley himself. *Catharine* might have had as its motto the sub-title from Fanny Burney's *Evelina,* "The History of a Young Lady's Entrance into the World," and perhaps it remained unfinished because Jane Austen did not yet know enough of the world Catharine was about to enter. An attempt to treat the mysterious and perplexing world beyond the horizons of Catharine—and of Jane Austen—had to wait for *Lady Susan.*

The case for *Lady Susan* as a crucial landmark in Jane Austen's artistic development was summed up by Reginald Farrer, in an article which remains—after almost fifty years—the best single introduction to her fiction. Farrer argues that "the cold unpleasantness of *Lady Susan* is but the youthful exaggeration of that irreconcilable judgment which is the very backbone of Jane Austen's power, and which, harshly evident in the first book, is the essential strength of all the later ones, finally protruding its bony structure nakedly again in *Persuasion.*" [46]

And one of the best of the recent critics, Marvin Mudrick, echoes Farrer when he asserts that *Lady Susan* is "uniquely characteristic of its author." [47] I agree that *Lady Susan* is an important work which must be understood in relation to Jane Austen's total achievement, but my estimate of its importance differs from those of Farrer and Mudrick.

Any assessment of *Lady Susan* must depend in large measure on the place assigned to this work in the sequence of composition. Mudrick is so anxious to prove *Lady Susan's* "centrality" that he reserves his analysis until after he has treated the first three major novels, even though he acknowledges that *Lady Susan* was probably written before 1801 and "is a consummation of the same hard unapologetic attitudes so individually embodied in the *Juvenilia* and, probably, in *Elinor and Marianne* and *First Impressions*" [the lost originals of *Sense and Sensibility* and *Pride and Prejudice*].[48] But to discuss *Lady Susan* after *Northanger Abbey*, *Sense and Sensibility*, and *Pride and Prejudice* must inevitably lead to distortion; for the most we can say of *Lady Susan* is that it was central to Jane Austen's artistic evolution in the 1790's, and that she still felt enough interest in it to make a fair copy sometime around 1805, the date of watermarks in the surviving manuscript. *Lady Susan* bears so little resemblance to the only other work known to have been composed between 1801 and 1809, *The Watsons*,[49] and is so close in style and attitude to the more sophisticated of the *Juvenilia* (especially "The Three Sisters," "Lesley Castle," and the third letter in "A Collection of Letters"), that we may accept the opinion of the authors of the *Life* that it was written in 1794 or 1795, probably just before the composition of *Elinor and Marianne*.[50] We know that *Elinor and Marianne*, like *Lady Susan*, was cast in the epistolary form,[51] which Jane Austen was never to use again. Indeed, the conclusion to *Lady Susan*, with its hurried tidying-up of the plot, opens with a jibe at the epistolary methods

("This Correspondence, by a meeting between some of the Parties & a separation between the others, could not, to the great detriment of the Post office Revenue, be continued longer"), and one is tempted to accept Mary Lascelles's suggestion that the Conclusion was added years after the composition of the letters, perhaps near the time of the fair copy, "when Jane Austen had lost patience with the device of the novel-in-letters." [52]

It is hard to resist the theory that *Lady Susan* had its origin in Jane Austen's personal experience, either in her observations of her cousin (later sister-in-law) Eliza de Feuillide or in family gossip about a lady similar to Lady Susan. [53] But if the original impulse lay in direct experience, the working out of Lady Susan's character seems peculiarly "literary." [54] The setting is not quite contemporary, the manners and motives belong more to the world of Richardson or the early Fanny Burney than to the world Jane Austen knew in the 1790's. Lady Susan differs from the predatory females of the later fiction in her thoroughgoing *hypocrisy*, and the fact that we can use this term—instead of duplicity or insincerity—points to an eighteenth-century milieu. Lady Susan is too consistently herself to be believable in the world of Jane Austen's other works; she would be out of place in any of the novels, for she is the only character in Jane Austen's fiction who is completely free of self-deception and illusion. It is as if Jane Austen, possessed by the need to present an amoral woman of the world, could not find in the society she knew the proper manners to clothe her creation, and therefore borrowed them from the literature of earlier decades. For it is the strength of Jane Austen's art that as she matured and her observation widened, she realized that women like Lady Susan are ideal creations, perhaps as far removed from reality as the Man of Feeling, and that no believable character would be so self-assured and so free from illusion.

The term "hypocrisy" has, as one of its root meanings, "the acting of a part on a stage," and Lady Susan's success is the direct result of her consummate talents as an actress. She can seldom be faulted because she has perfected herself at the art of simulation, and she can disguise her basic self-interest because she has mastered, through shrewd observations, the roles society assigns to its women. She can impersonate any part required of her, and because hers is the world of art—rather than of natural feeling—she possesses a tremendous advantage over those around her.

Since Lady Susan's hypocrisy involves a complete contrast between her outer appearance and her inner feelings, the epistolary form is well suited to recording her career. Through the letters to her London friend and confidante, Mrs. Johnson, we are informed of her true feeling and intentions, while the letters of those around her provide a running account of her social behavior. As a result we are placed in an admirable position for estimating the success or failure of her "acting," and we can appreciate, like a theatrical audience, the dramatic irony of the situations. It is not long before we discover the mainsprings of Lady Susan's actions: self-interest on the one hand, a code of sophisticated behavior on the other. In her own interest Lady Susan is careful never to violate overtly the social norms, for she must work out her own destiny within the framework of approved behavior. Consequently she and Mrs. Johnson, without irony or insincerity, can discuss the points of "honour" which she must observe (Letter 9). Lady Susan is perpetually conscious that her position in life depends on a scrupulous observance of appearances, no matter how much she may try to achieve liberty behind these appearances. Her casual reference to "Propriety & so forth" (Letter 31) is a simple acknowledgment of the limitations to her freedom.

Much of our sense of Lady Susan's dominating and frustrating presence comes from the repetition of certain words,

especially "anxiety," "deceit," "artifice," and "artfulness." In
Lady Susan Jane Austen is working within a rigid Art-Nature
antithesis almost as constricting as that of Mrs. Inchbald's *Nature and Art* (1796), in which all motives are reduced to natural benevolence or cunning artifice. But Jane Austen is too
sophisticated to falsify probable behavior on the side of Nature, she is free of Mrs. Inchbald's Godwinian ideas, and Lady
Susan's artifice is shown as remarkably effective. In successive
letters (Nos. 17 and 18) Catherine Vernon contrasts Lady
Susan's artful command of dissimulation with the daughter's
"artless affection" and "natural abilities"; while in the next
letter Lady Susan tells her confidante of Frederica's "artless"
behavior, which affords

> . . . the most reasonable hope of her being ridiculed & de-
> spised by every Man who sees her.
> Artlessness will never do in Love matters, & that girl is born
> a simpleton who has it either by nature or affectation.

This explicit and rather crude use of an Art-Nature contrast is
another sign that *Lady Susan* was of "literary" origin. In her
later fiction Jane Austen never makes the antithesis quite so
simple, and she embodies it in the dramatic actions of her
characters in such a way that Mrs. Inchbald's crude distinctions are left far behind.

The importance of *Lady Susan*, as I have already suggested,
is inflated by all those critics who see Jane Austen's irony as a
ruthless and dispassionate instrument, and who feel that most
of her later works are a shying away from the hard social realities embodied in Lady Susan. Marvin Mudrick sums up this
position at the end of his extended analysis of the work:

> The ultimate, tragic victim is Lady Susan, the beautiful woman
> who must waste her art in pretense, her passion in passing se-
> ductions, her will on invertebrates like her daughter and

Reginald; who—in a moment of sardonic self-revelation—drops everyone else and the gratifying efforts of virtuosity to marry Sir James Martin, the greatest booby of all, yet as usable as, and so little different from, the rest. Energy, in her immobile bounded conventional world, turns upon and devours itself. The world defeats Lady Susan, not because it recognizes her vices, but because her virtues have no room in it.[55]

There is obviously some truth in this view of the work. Lady Susan is attractive because of her passion and awareness, she is by far the most compelling figure in the story, and when she declares to Mrs. Johnson, "I am again myself;—gay and triumphant" (291), our reaction is one of momentary admiration, a tribute to self-possession and determination. But to make Lady Susan a tragic heroine, driven to her deceits by a "hollow" society, is to misread the whole work. Having undertaken a task beyond the range of her developing talent, and having established the mechanical oppositions of Art and Nature, Jane Austen found herself without a means for controlling the moral judgments of her readers. The epistolary form precluded any significant authorial comment, yet her irony had not evolved to a point where she could establish a presiding moral vision by implication. The result is a tug-of-war in which the reader's sympathy ultimately goes to the most vital character, and in which the author finds it impossible to make the badly needed social and moral discriminations. Jane Austen's recognition of failure is reflected in the abrupt breaking-off of the letters and the inadequate Conclusion. It would seem that in *Lady Susan* she undertook a subject beyond her technical control; and rather than demanding a reassessment of her succeeding fiction, *Lady Susan* emphasizes the rapidity of her artistic growth. The direction taken by Jane Austen's art after *Lady Susan* was not one of evasion but of exploration.

One corollary of the critical position that presents *Sense and*

Sensibility as a shying away from the harsh social facts confronted in *Lady Susan,* and *Mansfield Park* as a craven rejection of them, is a high estimate of *Lady Susan's* literary quality. Mudrick seems to imply that if *Lady Susan* is not as great
as the first three major novels, then this is partly due to lack of
revision.[56] Apparently the assumption is that *Lady Susan* must
possess a great artistic potential because it deals directly with
the social realities treated more obliquely in the later works;
and Jane Austen's abandonment of the piece is explained on
grounds of conformity or cowardice. But it should be obvious
that *Lady Susan,* in terms of style and narrative technique, is
neither as brilliant as *Love and Freindship* nor as promising as
Catharine. It is a dead end, an interesting but unsuccessful experiment in a dying form based upon outmoded manners; and
after its composition the problems posed in the *Juvenilia,* still
unresolved, remained as challenges to Jane Austen's maturing
art.

So far in this chapter we have examined the early works as
stages in a process of exploration, during the course of which
Jane Austen "roughed in" the social world of her major novels
and discovered many of her characteristic themes. Yet this
search for congenial subjects and a comprehensive moral out-
look was also a quest for stylistic and narrative techniques adequate to express them, and any consideration of the themes of
the *Juvenilia* must lead to an assessment of the young Jane
Austen's attitudes toward language and style, toward narrative
method, and toward the general form of the novel. For it is
against these early positions that we measure the later development of her art.

The parodies of the *Juvenilia* are so wide-ranging that we
have little difficulty in determining Jane Austen's early stylistic
ideals. Her natural talent for imitating the idioms of real life
is implicit in her remarkable ability at reproducing the ab-

surdities of dialogue which marked the popular fiction of the day. Many years later, in complaining of her niece's use of the phrase "vortex of Dissipation," she commented:

> I do not object to the Thing, but I cannot bear the expression; it is such thorough novel slang—and so old, that I dare say Adam met with it in the first novel he opened.[57]

In the *Juvenilia* Jane Austen tested her own ear for the varieties of probable conversation through her parodies of current "novel slang." A neat survey of the stylistic criticisms that dominate the early *Juvenilia* may be found in essay No. 59 of *The Loiterer* (March 1790), which was written by Henry Austen and his close friend Benjamin Portal. This ironic summary of the "Rules for *Prose Composition*" is a compendium of those affectations in style and manner which were ridiculed in the Austen household; it both reveals Jane Austen's debt to the family habit of ironic criticism and suggests that her own influence on the composition of *The Loiterer* may have been substantial. Jane Austen was certainly planning *Love and Freindship* while Henry was cataloguing the "occult principles of the science of composition."

Loiterer No. 59 first considers the function of style:

> Thanks to our elaborate predecessors, thoughts are easily collected on any subject: All that remains for us is, to disguise the expression yet preserve the substance, to introduce them however unconnected without obvious abruptness, and join them however little related without obvious incongruity. To this end it will be necessary to polish the style till the flaws in the interior of the piece are lost in the lustre of the surface; for the radiance of ornamental expression diffuses itself over every void, and blends the motley parts into one uniform and splendid whole.

The authors of the essay continue by demanding "that the sentence should principally be constructed of such words as boast Greek or Latin genealogy: however trivial this may seem to superficial judges, I venture to pronounce it a rule which admits not a single exception."

> For instance, *Ardour* should be preferred to *Heat—tardy* to *slow—sinuous* to *winding:* I should have little hope of an author who should write, "the country lying round," when he might so classically phrase it, "the country circumjacent." A great master of language of my acquaintance invariably uses "Fortitude" to the exclusion of "Magnanimity," as being nearer the latin by one letter.

But a "classical" vocabulary is not the only requisite for style. Attention must be given to the structure of the sentence.

> The cavalcade of sentences is most striking, when a row of Nouns is drawn up in the front and rear; and the period moves with a pretty ambling pace, when it's several Substantives are mounted on stately Adjectives. Hence my readers will easily conclude that they must never compress an idea into one word which may be diffused through two. . . . A band of proper names enters with great dignity into a sentence; and there are enough ready to enlist in any cause. In the selection of them regard should be principally had to Alliteration; and here Antithesis may be studied with great effect. . . . Among many [epithets], I cannot but point out to my readers, "the Judicious Blackstone," as the most happy resolution of plain Judge Blackstone which human ingenuity could invent.

· · · · ·

To please the ear, therefore, is the last and grand effort of a highly finished Style. To this end no labour must be considered too great, no attention too minute. The easiest way perhaps of attaining such an excellence will be to note down the most admired sentences of Addison, Junius, and Blair; to calculate the words in each member; the proportion of vowels to consonants; the balance of long and short syllables;—till your ear be so attuned to one particular measure, that your ideas may be spontaneously absorbed into the same revolving eddy of recursive harmony. Wherever there is any danger of sinking beneath the weight of your subject; your language should be proportionably swoln, and sublime; a full band is a wonderful support to a weak voice.

Having thus defined the proper style, the authors of the essay turn to "the conduct of a Piece." Here they state the general rule of composition that "the more obvious these truths are, the better," and insist that every obvious truth should be supported by "Mythological allusions" and "Authorities." But beyond this, they maintain that the skillful writer leaves nothing to his readers' imaginations:

> When he presents any image with which he wishes to depress his reader, he previously gives him his cue, by phrases similar to these: "It is melancholy to reflect;" "It is a painful and humiliating consideration."—When on the contrary he wishes to elevate him; he begins, something in this manner— "We gaze with sensible delight on this bright and amiable picture;" "From this gloomy catalogue we turn with eagerness to a more pleasing retrospect."

Behind the formula for "correct" style mocked in *Loiterer* No. 59 and the *Juvenilia* we can discern that clear sense of proper style—based on a perceptive critique of contemporary fiction—which was to govern Jane Austen's serious compositions. Mary Lascelles has said that Jane Austen appears to us "like one who inherits a prosperous and well-ordered estate— the heritage of a prose style in which neither generalization nor abstraction need signify vagueness, because there was close enough agreement as to the scope and significance of

such terms." [58] There is obviously some truth in this claim.
Like Dr. Johnson, Jane Austen is capable of using the abstract
vocabulary of eighteenth-century morality and aesthetics with
maximum precision, although we may doubt if the general
"agreement as to the scope and significance of such terms" was
ever as close as Miss Lascelles suggests.[59] But the quotation is
misleading in its implication that Jane Austen possessed one
"prose style," and that this is the style of her fiction. In fact
she was the master of several separate and identifiable styles,
the three most important being:

1. The generalized "Johnsonian" style of the essay periodi-
cals, a style well suited for moral and aesthetic judgments.

2. A "pre-Romantic" style drawn from Cowper, Gilpin, and
the more probable novels of sensibility.

3. The "real language of men," the various idioms used in
her own society and the fictitious world of her characters.

Of course I do not mean to imply by this schematic description that these various "styles" ever appear in pure form: (1)
and (2) are primarily the vehicles for her commentary, (3) the
substance of her dialogue; yet Jane Austen is capable of authorial comments in the modern idiom of the drawing room,
while some of her characters (such as Darcy) speak naturally
in a language somewhat out of fashion. But these "styles" do
have a certain reality as sub-strata of her prose, and we shall
see later that much of Jane Austen's precision and subtlety
stems from her consciousness of these "styles" and her ability
to merge or separate them at will. For with Jane Austen, as
with all novelists of manners, living itself is a matter of style,
and the idioms of the characters—and of the author—are often
our best guides to the careful discriminations of meaning and
purpose upon which the fiction depends.

Throughout Jane Austen's early work the major style of
authorial comment is the measured, generalized idiom of the
eighteenth-century essayists, the language of *The Rambler*

and *The Idler*. In her later novels it becomes muted and subtly transformed, losing much of its heaviness while retaining its moral precision; but in Jane Austen's letters the "Johnsonian" style remained to the last her chief means of quickly and intelligibly passing judgment on the life around her. For an example of this style, from midway through her career, we may take a passage from a letter of 1804 in which Jane Austen is conveying to Cassandra her opinion of a new acquaintance: "I do not perceive wit or genius, but she has sense and some degree of taste, and her manners are very engaging." [60] These general terms would have immediately communicated to Cassandra a fairly comprehensive moral and social judgment, and when we gloss the passage from Johnson's dictionary its precision becomes apparent. Similarly, when Jane Austen states in *Pride and Prejudice* that Mary Bennet had "neither genius nor taste" (25), we are expected to understand a great deal more than most modern readers *do* understand when confronted with these catchwords of eighteenth-century aesthetics. R. W. Chapman has done a great service for the reader of Jane Austen in his comments on words or expressions that have undergone radical changes in meaning since the eighteenth century,[61] but the problem of understanding her general terms is more than one of shifting usage. Her language was written for an audience familiar with the vocabulary of eighteenth-century moral and aesthetic discussion, and we must perform an act of historical understanding before her typical comments will give up their original burden of general yet precise meaning. In her early parodies Jane Austen's mockery is often directed at absurd abuses of the Johnsonian method, at empty abstractions and false antitheses:

> Tho' Benevolent & Candid, she was Generous & sincere; Tho' Pious & Good, she was Religious & amiable, & Tho' Elegant & Agreable, she was Polished & Entertaining.[62]

But these ironic hits only confirm her commitment to the genuine style, and in the more mature *Catharine* Jane Austen makes delicate and sincere use of such terms as Understanding, Taste, and Judgment to discriminate between the heroine and Camilla Stanley.

One of the most striking qualities of Jane Austen's mature prose is its lack of figurative language, and this can be traced in part to a reaction against the stock metaphors of the "land of fiction." Yet the scarcity of imagery and metaphor in her novels was more than a reaction against the excesses of poetic diction. She preferred general terms for the same reason as Dr. Johnson, because they could express her moral judgments; [63] but although her comments are usually general and her settings spare (in a letter of 1814, criticizing the fiction of her niece, she complained of overly minute and particular description [64]), her dialogue derives its strength from minute and particular observation. Specific, circumstantial, detailed, the speech of her characters is highly individual. In her mature fiction the generality of the comment is balanced against a particularity of subject and dialogue, thus creating a form that brings both the universal and the local into focus. Constructing her characters out of countless realistic details which are embodied in the dialogue, she judges them in general language which assumes a universal moral standard. And in doing this she resolves the conflict between moralist and historian which vitiated so much eighteenth century fiction.

Just as the verbal parodies of the *Juvenilia* reflect Jane Austen's dissatisfaction with the language of contemporary fiction, and foreshadow the future development of her own style, so the burlesques of improbable narrative method illuminate her growing sense of the novel's proper form. In the early *Juvenilia* she ridicules unmotivated narrative digressions ("Jack & Alice"), the sentimental heroine's compulsion to "tell her own story" (*Love and Freindship*), the crude handling of time

("Weeks & Fortnights flew away . . ."), plot improbabilities (". . . she fortunately perceived in a Corner of her Cell, a small saw & Ladder of ropes"), and the monotonous insertions of "(said she)" and "(replied I)." [65] One persistent line of criticism is directed at the epistolary novel, which had reached its peak of popularity at the time of her early experiments.[66] In "Amelia Webster" (*Volume the First*) the short and uninformative letters are an ironic commentary on the tediousness of the typical epistolary novel; there is also burlesque of the inevitable difficulties of communication ("I have found a very convenient old hollow oak to put our Letters in . . .") and the monotonous conventions (". . . but my Paper reminds me of concluding"). In other of the *Juvenilia* Jane Austen shows her awareness of the epistolary novel's tendency to collapse into a first-person journal, full of letters from "The Same to the Same." But she was also aware of the advantages of the form, its ability to present a number of viewpoints with tolerable authority, and in *Lady Susan* she uses the epistolary method with a variety and cleverness rarely equaled in the eighteenth century; yet even here the form did not satisfy her, and *Lady Susan* was finally ended with an impatient thrust at the epistolary restrictions. Perhaps the most satisfying example of Jane Austen's experimentation with the novel-in-letters is "The Three Sisters," where the form (two young ladies writing to their confidantes) shows signs of developing into a more subtle narrative structure, with Georgiana as the "central intelligence."

But the epistolary form was only one of the many narrative methods Jane Austen explored in her early works. Through imitation and burlesque she tested the range of the conventional forms, and finding herself unable to express her maturing view of the world completely in any one of them she gradually moved toward a narrative method of her own which would synthesize commentary and drama, objective judgment and subjective reactions. Many influences converged in the making of this new form: bourgeois theater, the periodical essay, Fanny Burney's domestic fiction, Richardson's attempts to chronicle the individual consciousness, the "immediacy" of the novel of sensibility. Most of these influences are fairly obvious, and we shall return to them in succeeding chapters as we trace the evolution of Jane Austen's narrative techniques. But the positive value of the novel of sensibility may need some explanation in the light of Jane Austen's juvenile ridicule of the form. In speaking of Henry Mackenzie, author of *The Man of Feeling*, Sir Walter Scott singled out his "principal object" as the establishment of a "tone of moral pathos" by "representing the effect of incidents, whether important or trifling, upon the human mind"; and later in the same essay Scott claimed that Mackenzie's works were "rather the history of effects produced on the human mind by a series of events, than the narrative of those events themselves." [67] Scott's comments should serve to remind us that the late eighteenth-century novels of sensibility, dreadful as they may have been, did perpetuate Richardson's interest in recording "an immediate impression of every circumstance," [68] and that alongside all the things Jane Austen learned *not* to do from the novelists of sensibility we should place her sincere interest in their efforts —however misguided and uncontrolled—to record the "effects produced on the human mind by a series of events," rather than "the narrative of those events themselves."

In order to achieve her quiet revolution in narrative method Jane Austen had to react vigorously against the accepted notions of the novel's artistic merit, and against the popular belief in its pernicious moral influence. The general disrepute of the genre at the time when she began writing may be judged from the hesitancy of the serious artist to accept the title "Novelist." In the Preface to her *Evelina* (1778) Fanny Burney acknowledged that, of all writers, the novelists are "more numerous but less respectable," and she took great pains to distinguish her work from that of her contemporaries; by the time *Camilla* was ready for publication (1796) she regretted having to call the work "a novel." [69] And in the "Advertisement" to her *Belinda* (1801) Maria Edgeworth flatly rejected the role of "Novelist."

> Every author has a right to give what appellation he may think proper to his works. The public have also a right to accept or refuse the classification that is presented.
>
> The following work is offered to the public as a Moral Tale —the author not wishing to acknowledge a Novel.

C. L. Thomson is probably right in her suggestion that the outright defense of novel-reading in *Northanger Abbey* is Jane Austen's reaction to this Advertisement; [70] certainly she would have been outraged by Maria Edgeworth's timid rejection of the title "Novelist." For Jane Austen, who had the good fortune to be reared in a family who were "great Novel-readers & not ashamed of being so," [71] shows in her earliest work a conviction of the genre's potential seriousness and flexibility that is in marked contrast to the common opinion of her age. She saw the form's possibilities so clearly because she realized that the popular objections were based on false distinctions and bad examples; and so successfully did she follow her conviction of the novel's possibilities that Bishop Whately's 1821 review of her works could open with the statement that "the times seem to be past when an apology was requisite from reviewers for condescending to notice a novel," and could go on to attribute this change not so much to a shift in public taste but to a radical alteration in the kind of fiction being produced. [72] Of course Jane Austen was not alone in promoting this new assessment of the novel's worth—Scott and Maria Edgeworth had a greater popular impact—but in retrospect we can see that she was the first to work from a renewed faith in the novel's potentialities as an art form.

If we are to appreciate the magnitude and importance of this revaluation we must examine the causes for the disrepute into which the novel had fallen after the great age of Fielding and Richardson. Some of these causes were inherent in the social and literary conditions of the time: a lack of great talents, the rapid expansion of the reading public, the enormous influence of the circulating libraries. But, as I suggested at the beginning of this chapter, the chief reason for the degeneration of the novel in the late eighteenth century was the lack of a coherent theory of fiction that could direct the development of the genre and defend it against purely moralistic objections. The great novelists of mid-century imposed their works on the age, over the attacks of the moralists, by the force of their talent; but only Fielding left a body of theoretical writing, and his criticism could give little help to Fanny Burney and her contemporaries. So, lacking a sense of direction and coerced by the popular demand for sentimental fictions, the typical late eighteenth-century novelist was helpless before the moralistic objections which had always been raised against the novel.

The definitive statement of these caveats was made by Johnson in *Rambler* No. 4 (March 1750), a short essay which was to have an immense—and retrograde—impact on the development of prose fiction. In this essay Johnson lent the weight of his authority to the commonplace opinion that the novel, since it thrives on plausibility and pretends to present life "as it is," exercises a greater influence over the mind (and especially the young mind) than the romance, which is patently improbable. Although pleased with the realism of the new form, and acknowledging that "the greatest excellency of art [is] to imitate nature," Johnson believed that we must "distinguish those parts of nature, which are most proper for imitation. . . ." He felt that the novel would have a power to corrupt in proportion to its success at social realism, and he concluded that faithful imitation is not sufficient justification; there must be regard for education and strict control of moral influence.

Johnson's remarks on the art of fiction in *Rambler* No. 4 represent but one side of his ambivalent and shifting attitude toward the nature of artistic "truth." The more liberal views of the imitative process found in his *Preface to Shakespeare* were never applied to the novel, and the shabby novels of sensibility seemed to justify the narrow moralism of *Rambler* No. 4. For half a century Johnson's strictures helped to prevent new speculation on the novel's form and range. In her *Progress of Romance* (1785), the most important extended treatment of the novel between 1770 and 1800, Clara Reeve echoed Johnson's argument; Fanny Burney is obviously disturbed by it in her uneasy Preface to *Evelina*; and the author of the article on the "Novel" in the 1797 edition of the *Encyclopaedia Britannica*, although an admirer of the genre, felt compelled to quote *Rambler* No. 4 at length. Obviously Johnson's arguments were still potent at the end of the century.

What was needed to counteract the popular distrust typified by Johnson's essay was a formal defense of the novel on aesthetic grounds. But the average late eighteenth-century novelist, instead of meeting the moralistic objections squarely, chose the lame defense of historicity. Fanny Burney refers to herself as merely the "editor" of *Evelina,* and one study of the late eighteenth-century novel lists over seventy titles which begin: *The History of. . . .* Something of the same impulse led Mrs. Radcliffe, whose sense of literary tact was quite high, to resolve all her fantastic effects into the "possible" or "natural" at the end of her stories, rather than rely on the logic of her created illusions. And as long as the supporters of the novel continued to accept the premises of their opponents, all their arguments remained makeshift and unconvincing.

From the very first Jane Austen stood free of this defensive attitude—indeed she satirizes it in the *Juvenilia*—and her early works reflect the gradual formulation of a rationale for the novel which could withstand all the Johnsonian objections. Crucial to her developing notion of the novel's potentialities was her rejection of *la belle nature*, nature refined or purified. In effect Jane Austen challenged the established view of how morality gets into fiction; instead of exercising her moral judgment in the suppression of certain details and the exaltation of others, she vested it in the manner of their treatment. Her implied answer to all moralistic criticism of fiction was that the influence of art—for good or for evil—lies not in the matter it imitates but in the forms of expression. By demonstrating that the novelist can combine absolute fidelity to the details of life (Scott compared her art to "Flemish painting") with the maintenance of a consistent moral viewpoint, Jane Austen salvaged fiction from slavish subservience to its audience and re-established it as an independent form. The early reviews of her work, especially those by Scott and Whately, although they are intensely concerned with the novel as moral example, show a new recognition of the genre's complexity and subtlety. Jane Austen applied to the novel the same liberal concepts of truth and imitation that her great contemporaries were applying to poetry, and in doing so she anticipated the central arguments of Henry James's classic essay, "The Art of Fiction." [73] But this is a theme for the chapters to come.

II

THE SYMPATHETIC
IMAGINATION

Northanger Abbey and *Sense and Sensibility*

Viewed as a whole, *Northanger Abbey* is certainly the earliest of Jane Austen's major works.[1] Although it was begun in 1798 after the first drafts of *Sense and Sensibility* and *Pride and Prejudice* had been written, both of these novels underwent radical revision shortly before their publication in 1811 and 1813, while Jane Austen's *Advertisement* to *Northanger Abbey* states that it was "finished in the year 1803." There is some possibility that the novel was touched up after 1803, but these revisions could not have been extensive; and we are justified in taking *Northanger Abbey* as the only major work that was completely a product of the first half of Jane Austen's career. Certainly all the evidence of style and narrative method points toward an early date: many of the characters are two-dimensional, and Jane Austen never seems quite sure of her relationship to Henry Tilney. She frequently allows him to usurp her authority, to voice her judgments and wield her irony, and the result is considerable ambiguity concerning her attitude toward the novel's "hero." But if *Northanger Abbey* lacks the narrative sophistication of the later works it does not lack their complexity of theme, and it would be a mistake to think that Jane Austen is manipulating a straightforward contrast between Gothic nonsense and "the common feelings of common life" (19). If she started out to expose the absurdities of Gothic fiction she ended by exposing much more, and any analysis of *Northanger Abbey* must begin with an examination of the relation between the subplot (Catherine's reading of Gothic novels and its impact on her behavior) and the work's main action. For in learning to handle the fictions of the Gothic world Catherine comes to recognize the other fictions which haunt her life.

A close reading of the subplot in *Northanger Abbey* suggests that it may not have been a part of Jane Austen's original plan.[2] The chapters devoted mainly to literary burlesque and parody (I–II, XX–XXV) form detachable units, and the other references to Gothic fiction and Catherine's role as a "heroine" could easily have been inserted into the original story of Catherine's entrance into the world. But whether the subplot developed as part of the author's original intention, or whether it was added later to reinforce the main action, the artistic impact is the same; and the Gothic elements are a brilliant commentary on Catherine's general character and behavior.

The era of the Gothic novel's greatest popularity was amazingly brief: it began in the early 1790's, reached its peak with the publication of *The Mysteries of Udolpho* (1794) and *The Monk* (1796), and started to decline shortly after the publication of Mrs. Radcliffe's *The Italian* in 1797. One of the first signs of this decline in popularity was the appearance of a series of burlesques and satires, ranging from *The Rovers* (a four-act burlesque in the *Anti-Jacobin* for 1798) through Maria Edgeworth's *Angelina* (1801) to E. S. Barrett's *The Heroine* (1813).[3] Although *Northanger Abbey* was not published until six months after its author's death in 1817, and

Jane Austen had felt compelled in 1816 to apologize for "those parts of the work which thirteen years have made comparatively obsolete," [4] at the time of the first draft *Northanger Abbey* was a pioneer criticism of the Gothic form, once more demonstrating Jane Austen's extraordinary grasp of current literary trends and opinions. She was always among the first to recognize the decay of a literary form, and to see in the lifeless conventions a field for irony. In *Northanger Abbey* she could write a recipe for the conventional "heroine," and then invert this formula to produce her Catherine, simply because the average Gothic fiction had become a standard mixture of familiar ingredients. The *Magasin encyclopédique* for 1797 printed the following *"Recipe"* for "a good mixture of shudders and fright, in three volumes":

> An old castle, half of it crumbling down,
> A long corridor, with numerous doors many of which must be hidden,
> Three corpses still weltering in their blood,
> Three skeletons carefully wrapped up,
> An old woman hanged, stabbed several times in her throat,
> Robbers and ruffians galore,
> A sufficient dose of whispers, stifled moans and frightful din.

> All those ingredients well mixed and divided into three parts or volumes give an excellent mixture which all those who have no black blood may take just before going to bed while having their baths. They will feel all the better for it. Probatum est.[5]

The impossibility of locating a single "source" for the Gothic elements in *Northanger Abbey* testifies to this standardization of the form: Mary Lascelles finds in Catherine's behavior a point-by-point inversion of the career of Charlotte Smith's Emmeline, while C. L. Thomson believes that Jane Austen's model was the heroine of *Udolpho*.[6] Actually Catherine Morland is a mirror-image of the "standard" heroine, and the burlesque of *Northanger Abbey* depends in large measure on the virtual identity of all the Gothic heroines. Jane Austen's target was the form in general, not any particular thriller. We should remember that the Gothic novel was not a completely separate genre but rather an extension of the novel of sensibility, and that in the midst of the Black Forest or on the mountains of Sicily the stale conventions of sensibility still held true. In fact the terrors of the Gothic world were evoked in response to a need for situations that would work on the heroine's sensibility with greater violence than any to be met in the life of the Home Counties. German horror, anti-clericalism, and the native English graveyard tradition were all welded upon the novel of sensibility to produce the Gothic fiction of the 1790's. In his fine essay on "The Northanger Novels," Michael Sadleir has shown that Jane Austen was well read in this fiction, and keenly aware of the two divergent "schools": that of Monk Lewis, violent, revolutionary, shocking; and that of Mrs. Radcliffe, where the titillation of the audience depends not so much on the quality of the horrors as on the contrast between the secure world of the reader and the perilous world of the fiction.[7] As we shall see later, Jane Austen is primarily interested in the Gothicism of Mrs. Radcliffe, although she fairly divides Isabella's list of horrid fiction between the two schools.

It is important to place *Northanger Abbey* as part of a general reaction against Gothic conventions, but it is more important to note the differences between Jane Austen's method and that of the other anti-Gothic satires. Typical of these is Barrett's *The Heroine*, which Jane Austen thought "a delightful burlesque, particularly on the Radcliffe style."[8] In *The Heroine* the formula of the "Quixotic" novel is applied to the Gothic world; Barrett's heroine, her head stuffed with fictions, tries to impose her imaginary world on reality, and is continually rebuffed. But Jane Austen was too subtle to use this formula, which usually produced passages of broad burlesque alternating with obvious moralizing. Instead of creating a deluded young woman who considers herself a Gothic heroine forced to live in an alien environment, Jane Austen fashioned in Catherine Morland an "anti-heroine," whose early life is at every point the reverse of the classic heroine's; when Catherine is exposed to the influence of Gothic fiction she is not deluded into thinking herself a heroine, but rather into imagining that the world around her is inhabited by Gothic horrors. Thus she is never exposed to the charge of vanity or selfishness, and Jane Austen is able to use the Gothic subplot as a means of commenting on Catherine's education into reality. Of course there is a good deal of broad burlesque in *Northanger Abbey*, and some purely literary satire (especially in the Conclusion, where the gratuitous explanation for the origin of the laundry bills is a spoof on Mrs. Radcliffe's habit of relating every improbable event to "actuality"). But the "literary" interest in *Northanger Abbey* is much less than in the *Juvenilia*, and the Gothic motif is merely one movement—although an important one—in a complex drama of illusion and recognition.

I have said that although Jane Austen demonstrates a familiarity with both "schools" of Gothic fiction, her main concern is with that of Mrs. Radcliffe. This is because she plainly saw the complacency which underlay the form. Whereas Monk Lewis was dealing, however sensationally, with Byronic materials, and using Gothic devices to figure forth certain psychological truths, Mrs. Radcliffe deliberately fostered a sense of remoteness in her Gothic fictions. "She has uniformly selected the south of Europe for her place of action," said Scott, a locale where "passions, like the weeds of the climate, are supposed to attain portentous growth." [9] When Catherine Morland compares Bath's Beechen Cliff with the "south of France"— much to the surprise of Henry Tilney—she is speaking from broad fictional knowledge. The appeal of the Radcliffean novel was founded on the contrast between the dangers of the heroine's life and the security of the reader's, between the violence of Sicily and the tranquillity of Twickenham. Jane Austen understood this appeal to vicarious emotion, and was determined to expose both its basic sentimentality and fundamental unreality. Not only does the reader of Radcliffean fiction get her emotions at second hand, she indulges in the comforting illusion that violent passions are confined to alien landscapes. As Lionel Trilling has suggested, Catherine's belief in a violent and uncertain life lurking beneath the surface of English society is nearer the truth than the complacent conviction, shared by the readers of Mrs. Radcliffe, that life in the Home Counties is always sane and orderly.[10] General Tilney's actual abuse of Catherine is as bad in its way as anything she had imagined, and her flight from Northanger Abbey, alone and outcast, is an event straight from the Gothic repertory. Jane Austen's irony is not directed at Catherine's sympathetic imagination, but at her misuse of it; and the novel's deepest criticism is reserved for the average reader's complacent reaction to the exposure of Catherine's "folly." Those who read *Northanger Abbey* as a straightforward drama in which Sense conquers Sensibility, and the disordered Imagination is put to flight by Reason, are neglecting the novel's ultimate irony.

A good example of Jane Austen's subtle handling of illusion and reality may be found in the scene where Henry Tilney exploits Catherine's innocent remark that "something very shocking indeed, will soon come out in London." Eleanor Tilney has misunderstood Catherine's reference to the publication of a new "horrid" novel, and fears that some social "riot" is threatened. At this point Henry adjudicates:

> "My dear Eleanor, the riot is only in your own brain. The confusion there is scandalous. Miss Morland has been talking

of nothing more dreadful than a new publication which is shortly to come out, in three duodecimo volumes, two hundred and seventy-six pages in each, with a frontispiece to the first, of two tombstones and a lantern—do you understand?—And you, Miss Morland—my stupid sister has mistaken all your clearest expressions. You talked of expected horrors in London—and instead of instantly conceiving, as any rational creature would have done, that such words could relate only to a circulating library, she immediately pictured to herself a mob of three thousand men assembling in St. George's Fields; the Bank attacked, the Tower threatened, the streets of London flowing with blood, a detachment of the 12th Light Dragoons, (the hopes of the nation,) called up from Northampton to quell the insurgents, and the gallant Capt. Frederick Tilney, in the moment of charging at the head of his troop, knocked off his horse by a brickbat from an upper window. Forgive her stupidity. The fears of the sister have added to the weakness of the woman; but she is by no means a simpleton in general." (112–13)

On the surface this appears to be a lively and reasonable rebuke of Eleanor's borrowed terrors; the riot which Henry describes so graphically seems absurd and unreal against the quiet background of Bath society. But in fact Henry is constructing his imaginary disaster out of the actual details of the 1780 Gordon Riots,[11] and the burden of the passage is not the comforting assurance that "it can't happen here." The ironies of this misunderstanding are directed at complacent sense as well as exaggerated sensibility, and the entire scene prefigures the time when Catherine's imaginary horrors at Northanger Abbey will yield to the real terrors of life.

When Henry Tilney discovers Catherine outside his mother's room, and learns of her suspicion that General Tilney murdered her, his first words are those of triumphant common-sense:

"Dear Miss Morland, consider the dreadful nature of the suspicions you have entertained. What have you been judging
from? Remember the country and the age in which we live. Remember that we are English, that we are Christians. Consult
your own understanding, your own sense of the probable, your
own observation of what is passing around you—Does our
education prepare us for such atrocities? Do our laws connive
at them?"

So far Henry's rebuke reflects the assumptions of the average
reader, an easy assurance that Gothic horror is alien to eighteenth-century England. But, as D. W. Harding has shrewdly
observed,[12] Henry's remarks gradually take on a more intricate
meaning.

"Could they [such atrocities] be perpetrated without being
known, in a country like this, where social and literary intercourse is on such a footing; where every man is surrounded by a
neighbourhood of voluntary spies, and where roads and news-
papers lay every thing open? Dearest Miss Morland, what ideas
have you been admitting?" (197–8)

Gothic violence is not impossible in English society, only repressed and rigidly controlled, and "a neighborhood of spies"
is hardly the description of an idyllic society. Jane Austen
might have said, with Henry James, "I have the imagination
of disaster and see life as ferocious and sinister."[13] Her criticism of Catherine's imagination is not that it is ridiculous or
dangerous *per se*, but that it is uncontrolled by judgment.
When the "alarms of romance" give way to the "anxieties of
common life" at Northanger, these anxieties are not less intense because of their foundation in probability; indeed, they
are "mournfully superior in reality and substance" (227). And
when Catherine learns the true motives for General Tilney's
outrageous behavior, she feels "that in suspecting General Til-

ney of either murdering or shutting up his wife, she had scarcely sinned against his character, or magnified his cruelty" (247). Jane Austen records this emotion with an irony which does not entirely invalidate it.

In the *"Recipe"* for a Gothic novel quoted earlier in this chapter the *Magasin encyclopédique* describes the formula as an excellent tonic for readers to take "just before going to bed while having their baths," and this is a perceptive observation on the sentimental bracketing of remote horrors and immediate comforts which characterized the Gothic craze. Like Byron and Monk Lewis, Jane Austen knew that the reader's feeling of cozy security was an illusion, and that the ridiculousness of the average Gothic fiction lay in its sentimentality and improbability, not in the emotions which it presented in debased form. Kenneth Clark has said that "every Romantic style reflects the daydream of its creators," a daydream which is, "in some measure, complementary to the real world."

> When life is fierce and uncertain the imagination craves for classical repose. But as society becomes tranquil, the imagination is starved of action, and the immensely secure society of the eighteenth century indulged in daydreams of incredible violence.[14]

Clark's generalization can easily be applied to the artificially restricted life of Catherine Morland, a life which fosters illusion. It was Jane Austen's purpose to destroy the daydream, but she refused to replace it with the greater illusion that all of life is probable and orderly. If she had intended to launch a full-scale ironic attack on the dangers of imagination, as some critics have claimed, she would have turned Catherine into the standard "heroine" of a Quixotic novel, self-confident, rebellious, an exaggerated figure of burlesque. But by making Catherine's self-delusion completely probable, by emphasizing her lack of pretension, and by integrating the literary satire into a classic tale of "education," Jane Austen acknowledged a larger aim. At its deepest level *Northanger Abbey* probes the virtues and limitations of what the eighteenth century would have called the sympathetic imagination, that faculty which promotes benevolence and generosity. Henry Tilney, who is never far from the author, is quick to discern this quality in Catherine's personality.

> "With you, it is not, How is such a one likely to be influenced? What is the inducement most likely to act upon such a person's feelings, age, situation, and probable habits of life considered?—but, how should *I* be influenced, what would be *my* inducement in acting so and so?" (132)

Now it seems clear that Jane Austen, in her life and in her art, was an admirer of the sympathetic imagination. It is the faculty which sweetens Catherine's character, the main source of Henry's affection. But Jane Austen also knew how easily such sympathy can be duped or deluded, and in *Northanger Abbey* she dramatized the dangers of uncontrolled sympathy. When untempered by judgment and reason the sympathetic imagination leads Catherine to her naïve mistakes in assessing both situation and character. Her projection of Gothic motives into the life at Northanger, and her misunderstanding of Isabella's nature, result from uncritical acceptance of fictions: in the one case the fictions of art are taken as reality, in the other the fictions of outward appearance are mistaken for the substance of character. The sympathetic imagination must be regulated; this is the sum of Catherine's education. She is cured of her illusions by being initiated into the real world, which is neither more nor less fierce than the fictional world, only different. In *Northanger Abbey* Jane Austen explored a problem to which she would return again and again, the problem of accommodating reason and feeling, of regulating sympathy without destroying it.

Stated in the abstract, the leading themes of *Northanger Abbey* sound as rich and subtle as those of Jane Austen's later works; but when we encounter them in the novel we find that their expression is hampered by lapses in tone and curious shifts in narrative method. We can isolate in *Northanger Abbey* most of the techniques that mark Jane Austen's greatest fiction, but they never coalesce into a satisfactory whole. What we miss is that sense of a controlling attitude which is part of the "atmosphere" in *Pride and Prejudice* or *Emma*. It is not that Jane Austen has difficulty in keeping herself out of the novel in *Northanger Abbey*—to say that would be to judge the work by the standards of a different kind of fiction. The real problem is inconsistency: some passages point forward to the dramatic ironies of the mature works, while others revert to the cruder methods of the *Juvenilia*. Typical of the latter is the famous "defence" of novel-reading in Chapter V:

> . . . I will not adopt that ungenerous and impolitic custom so common with novel writers, of degrading by their contemptuous censure the very performances, to the number of which they are themselves adding—joining with their greatest enemies in bestowing the harshest epithets on such works, and scarcely ever permitting them to be read by their own heroine, who, if she accidentally take up a novel, is sure to turn over its insipid pages with disgust. Alas! if the heroine of one novel be not patronized by the heroine of another, from whom can she expect protection and regard? I cannot approve of it. . . . "And what are you reading, Miss ———?" "Oh! it is only a novel!" replies the young lady; while she lays down her book with affected indifference, or momentary shame.—"It is only Cecilia, or Camilla, or Belinda;" or, in short, only some work in which the greatest powers of the mind are displayed, in which the most thorough knowledge of human nature, the happiest de-

lineation of its varieties, the liveliest effusions of wit and humour are conveyed to the world in the best chosen language.
Now, had the same young lady been engaged with a volume of
the Spectator, instead of such a work, how proudly would she
have produced the book, and told its name; though the chances
must be against her being occupied by any part of that volumi-
nous publication, of which either the matter or manner would
not disgust a young person of taste: the substance of its papers
so often consisting in the statement of improbable circumstances, unnatural characters, and topics of conversation, which
no longer concern any one living; and their language, too, frequently so coarse as to give no very favourable idea of the age
that could endure it. (37–8)

This is not a simple passage; although Jane Austen is obviously serious in attacking the craven attitudes of contemporary
novelists and their readers, she cannot resist the protective
irony of overstatement. What is jarring about the passage is
the intrusion of the author after we have come to accept
Henry Tilney as her spokesman. Henry's attitudes merge with
those of his creator on so many occasions that we are disturbed when she speaks to us directly, or when Henry is suddenly subjected to her irony. All this is but to say that Jane
Austen was experimenting in *Northanger Abbey* with several
narrative methods she had not fully mastered, and the result is
a lack of consistency in viewpoint. From time to time she confines our knowledge to Catherine's horizons, using her heroine
as a "center of consciousness," but Catherine's lack of intro-
spection prevents any consistent use of this technique. The
most sophisticated sections of the novel, and those that remind
us most strongly of the later novels, are the dramatic exchanges
where Jane Austen allows a character to expose his own nature
through word and gesture.

    Chapter XVIII provides a superb example of Jane Austen's
command of dramatic action. Here she confines herself to dia-

logue between Catherine and Isabella, to simple description, and to recording Catherine's naïve reactions; the author scarcely intrudes upon the scene, and our awareness of Isabella's changing opinions is derived entirely from her conversation. The opening sequence of action and dialogue—Isabella's choice of an "out of the way" bench which commands the whole room, her anxious glances, her indifference to James's possible appearance—is a clear indication to the reader of her changing attitudes. Her familiar reference to "Tilney" (in contrast with Catherine's "Mr. Tilney") confirms her new interest in him. And when Catherine, after disclaiming any special affection for John Thorpe, comforts Isabella with the reminder: "And, you know, we shall still be sisters," Isabella replies in a manner which makes her ambition obvious to the reader, if not to Catherine: "Yes, yes," (with a blush) "there are more ways than one of our being sisters.—But where am I wandering to?" (145). Isabella's conversation then dwells on the fickleness of young opinion, culminating in a quotation from Captain Tilney on the subject: "Tilney says, there is nothing people are so often deceived in, as the state of their own affections . . ." (147). At this point Captain Tilney enters the room, and his whispered exchange with Isabella makes the situation clear to all but Catherine, who evolves the naïve theory that Isabella is "unconsciously" encouraging Captain Tilney. The chapter ends with a fine passage in which Jane Austen records Catherine's troubled reactions to the scene she has just witnessed.

> It seemed to her that Captain Tilney was falling in love with Isabella, and Isabella unconsciously encouraging him; unconsciously it must be, for Isabella's attachment to James was as certain and well acknowledged as her engagement. To doubt her truth or good intentions was impossible; and yet, during the whole of their conversation her manner had been odd. She

wished Isabella had talked more like her usual self, and not so much about money; and had not looked so well pleased at the sight of Captain Tilney. How strange that she should not perceive his admiration! Catherine longed to give her a hint of it, to put her on her guard, and prevent all the pain which her too lively behaviour might otherwise create both for him and her brother.

The compliment of John Thorpe's affection did not make amends for this thoughtlessness in his sister. . . . Isabella talked of his attentions; *she* had never been sensible of any; but Isabella had said many things which she hoped had been spoken in haste, and would never be said again; and upon this she was glad to rest altogether for present ease and comfort. (148)

In this chapter we see Jane Austen moving toward that easy balance of dramatic action and psychological exposition—Henry James's "scene" and "picture"—which was to become the hallmark of her greatest fiction. Long before the reader comes to the *sotto voce* exchange between Isabella and Captain Tilney he is aware of the relationship which has developed between the two since their meeting at the dance, but Jane Austen has been careful to communicate this knowledge only through action and dialogue. Her own voice has been reserved for the recording of Catherine's naïve opinions, leaving the reader free to interpret the scene's dramatic irony. We are hardly conscious of Jane Austen's presence, yet she has retained control over our developing awareness. Such a complex method combines the effects of dramatic irony with the privilege of psychological interpretation, and allows us to regard the action both from Catherine's limited point-of-view and the author's omniscient perspective. But before this method could be confidently pursued on a large scale Jane Austen had to solve the structural problems that confronted her in *Northanger Abbey* and, more acutely, in *Sense and Sensibility*.

Most readers would agree that *Sense and Sensibility* is the least interesting of Jane Austen's major works. Like *Northanger Abbey* it is marred by inconsistencies in tone and point-of-view which reflect a fundamental uncertainty of conception, but it lacks the atmosphere of freshness and enthusiasm that redeems *Northanger Abbey*. The difficulties under which Jane Austen is laboring are obvious on almost every page. Yet in the pattern of her artistic development *Sense and Sensibility* occupies an important place; it bridges the two halves of her career, and poses the crucial problems which were later resolved in *Pride and Prejudice*. It is a classic example of the unsatisfactory work which reveals more, in some ways, than the masterpiece. Through the cracks and flaws of *Sense and Sensibility* we can discern—much more easily than in the polished surface of *Pride and Prejudice*—the problems Jane Austen encountered when she moved beyond burlesque and sought to reform the serious novel.

Many of the difficulties in *Sense and Sensibility* can be explained, if not excused, by an examination of its evolution. We know from the Austen-Leighs' *Life* that the original version of the novel, an epistolary work called *Elinor and Marianne*, was written around 1795–96, just before the composition of *First Impressions* (the early version of *Pride and Prejudice*) and shortly after the writing of *Lady Susan*. In her memorandum on the novels Cassandra Austen states that *Sense and Sensibility* was begun in November 1797, after the completion of *First Impressions*, and in his *Memoir of Jane Austen* J. E. Austen-Leigh claims that this version was the "final form." But clearly this cannot be true, for some of the literary allusions belong to a later decade, and the author of the *Memoir* speaks elsewhere of the novel's being revised and prepared for the press in 1809–10. How extensive this revision was it is hard to say. The names of two of the major characters may have been altered, and there are clear indications of stylistic revision. Some of the chapters (such as Chapter II) could hardly have been written before 1809, certainly not before the composition of *The Watsons* (*c.* 1803), since they demonstrate a dramatic ability equal to that found in *Pride and Prejudice.* Other chapters could easily have survived from the 1790's with few changes. Some of the long speeches suggest an imperfect assimilation of the original letters,[15] and the contrasts in style between adjacent passages are quite striking. A census of recurring general terms which are characteristic of Jane Austen's early expository prose (Judgment, Wit, Taste, Genius, and the like) revealed that they are not uniformly distributed throughout the novel. The sum of the evidence is that we must regard *Sense and Sensibility* as a youthful work patched up at a later date, in which the crude antitheses of the original structure were never successfully overcome. Part of the vitality of *Northanger Abbey* can be ascribed to the fact that Jane Austen began to work on it after completing the first drafts of *Sense and Sensibility* and *Pride and Prejudice,* and drove it to conclusion within a relatively short space of time. In *Sense and Sensibility* the later revisions did not strike deep enough to overcome the lack of continuity in the novel's composition.

The titles *Sense and Sensibility* and *Pride and Prejudice* derive from a standard thematic pattern set by late eighteenth-century moralistic fiction, in which opposed qualities of mind are dramatized through opposed personalities, usually sisters or close friends of radically different temperaments. Of course Jane Austen sought to modify this antithetical structure in creating *Sense and Sensibility,* and she transformed it almost beyond recognition in the final version of *Pride and Prejudice,* where it would be difficult to associate the hero with one particular quality and the heroine with its opposite. But the rigid antithetical form was her starting point in both novels, and in

Sense and Sensibility she never escaped from it; we are still justified in saying that Marianne represents Sensibility while Elinor stands for Sense. In *Sense and Sensibility* we witness that struggle between an inherited form and fresh experience which so often marks the transitional works of a great artist. In order to appreciate Jane Austen's advance over the conventional treatments of opposed temperaments, as well as her bondage to them, we can do no better than to compare *Sense and Sensibility* with a contemporary novel which handles the same theme in conventional fashion.

A number of foils suggest themselves—Mrs. Inchbald's *Nature and Art,* or Jane West's *A Gossip's Story,* which may have been one source for *Sense and Sensibility* [16]—but the most illuminating counterpart is provided by Maria Edgeworth's *Letters of Julia and Caroline,* which was published in 1795 at the time when Jane Austen was beginning work on her *Elinor and Marianne.*[17] I do not claim that the *Letters of Julia and Caroline* were a source for *Elinor and Marianne* (although Jane Austen must have read the work), but they do provide an index to the traditional treatment of Jane Austen's theme. Maria Edgeworth was strongly under the influence of Madame de Genlis's moralistic fiction, and in the *Letters* she formulates the distinctions between Sense and Sensibility in uncompromising terms.

In the exchange of letters, Julia speaks for Sensibility and Caroline is the epitome of Sense. In her first letter Julia presents the case for Sensibility in exaggerated form. She complains to Caroline that "you urge me to *think,* I profess only to *feel.*" [18] All Caroline's pleas for reflection and analysis are rejected:

> "Reflect upon my feelings!"—dear Caroline, is it not enough that I do feel?—All that I dread is that *apathy* which philosophers call tranquillity. You tell me that by continually *indulg-*

ing I shall weaken my natural sensibility; are not all the faculties of the soul improved, refined by exercise, and why shall *this* be excepted from the general law?

But I must not you tell me, indulge my taste for romance and poetry, lest I waste that sympathy on *fiction* which *reality* so much better deserves. My dear friend, let us cherish the precious propensity to pity! no matter what the object; sympathy with fiction or reality, arises from the same disposition. When the sigh of compassion rises in my bosom, when the spontaneous tear starts from my eye, what frigid moralist shall "stop the genial current of the soul," shall say to the tide of passion, *so far shalt thou go, and no farther?*—Shall man presume to circumscribe that which Providence has left unbounded? [19]

In this opening letter Julia formulates a choice between "the even temper, the poised judgment, the stoical serenity of philosophy," and the "eager genius, the exquisite sensibility of enthusiasm." She glories in the "amiable defects" of her attitude: *"Enthusiasm is my choice."* [20]

Caroline's reply to this effusion poses "fact against eloquence, philosophy against enthusiasm." [21] She sets out to examine Julia's "amiable defects" in rational fashion, and in a prose which is as restrained and dull as Julia's is gay and free. She argues that Julia's criterion of "pleasure" (the amiable woman, according to Julia, desires "to please") is based on vanity, and that the objects of a desire to please can only be selected by reason and judgment. She attacks indiscriminate exercises of sensibility as indulgences which blunt the genuine power of sympathy, and she makes a plea for prudent action.

These opening letters are a clear exposition of the popular "philosophic" defenses for Sense and Sensibility. The remaining letters are devoted to Julia's adventures, demonstrating in terms of real life the follies of unrestrained sentiment. Faced with a choice between two men who resemble Colonel Brandon and Willoughby, Julia ignores Caroline's advice and makes the wrong decision. We learn of the failure of Julia's marriage, her increasing moral confusion, her flight to the Continent with a lover, her penitent return, and her tragic death. As these disasters unfold Caroline's behavior is prudent, not to say prudish, and at the end of the *Letters* the moral is pounded home with unrelieved crudity. Julia dies a victim of her own sympathetic illusions, destroyed by her flight from reason.

Maria Edgeworth's *Letters of Julia and Caroline* gives us a clear sense of the rigid attitudes and inflexible antithetic structure which oppress Jane Austen in *Sense and Sensibility*. Although Miss Edgeworth accepts the traditional distinction between "natural sensibility" and "excessive sensibility," [22] and claims that Caroline is not deficient in the former (just as Jane Austen claims natural sensibility for Elinor), Julia and Caroline are stereotypes of opposed temperaments. And since they represent extremes, the working-out of their destinies leaves little room for realistic drama. Maria Edgeworth's antithesis is essentially a philosophic one, as rigorous as that made by Adam Smith in his *Theory of Moral Sentiments,* where the Stoical system of self-command is opposed to the Benevolent system of sympathetic indulgence. Now Jane Austen inherited from the eighteenth century this division between the ethic of rational experience and the ethic of natural feeling, and along with it she inherited the characteristic eighteenth-centry desire for an accommodation or compromise between the extremes. But she did not inherit a literary form for expressing such an accommodation, and in *Sense and Sensibility* we see her struggling against conventional (and improbable) stereotypes of character and action, searching for a flexible structure which will liberate her art from the tyranny of antithesis and give her complex moral vision adequate expression.

Not only did Jane Austen have to liberate herself from the

confines of stereotyped characterization and didactic action, she had to free herself from the language of antithesis. Take the following table of general terms, compiled from the *Letters of Julia and Caroline:*

Julia	Caroline
Feeling	Reason
Nature	Art
Freedom	System
Spontaneity	Reflection, Analysis
Fortune	Prudence
Indulgence	Self-Control
Enthusiasm	Philosophy
Sensibility	Sense, Judgment
Love	Esteem
Eloquence	Fact

This is the language of Sense and Sensibility, these are the terms of approbation and abuse; but they are all abstract statements of extremes.[23] Although we have noted how much Jane Austen appreciated the power of precise general language, and how finely she can balance abstract discourse against specific language, it must be acknowledged that in *Sense and Sensibility* her increasingly subtle discriminations struggle against the fixities of an antithetical vocabulary. Although admirably suited for the black-and-white world of burlesque, identifying tags such as "Sense" and "Sensibility" are obstacles to the maturing artist. The original epistolary version of *Sense and Sensibility* must have contained a broad satire on excessive sensibility, and in this it would have been greatly superior to Maria Edgeworth's *Letters of Julia and Caroline;* but the *Letters* do indicate the restrictive qualities of the language of contemporary fiction, the language Jane Austen had to use in her first attempts at a full-length novel. In *Sense and Sensibil-*

ity we often feel that the author is caught in the web of a language which tends to describe "types," not individuals. Obviously re-creation, rather than patchwork revision, would have been required to eradicate all signs of the novel's original schematic structure.

It is clear from Jane Austen's description of the two sisters in Chapter I that she hoped to avoid the traditional stereotypes of Sense and Sensibility.

> Elinor, this eldest daughter whose advice was so effectual, possessed a strength of understanding, and coolness of judgment, which qualified her, though only nineteen, to be the counsellor of her mother, and enabled her to counteract, to the advantage of them all, that eagerness of mind in Mrs. Dashwood which must generally have led to imprudence. She had an excellent heart;—her disposition was affectionate, and her feelings were strong; but she knew how to govern them: it was a knowledge which her mother had yet to learn, and which one of her sisters had resolved never to be taught.
>
> Marianne's abilities were, in many respects, quite equal to Elinor's. She was sensible and clever; but eager in every thing; her sorrows, her joys, could have no moderation. She was generous, amiable, interesting: she was every thing but prudent. The resemblance between her and her mother was strikingly great. (6)

Unfortunately, the sensitive discriminations of this passage are never completely embodied in the novel's action and dialogue. Although Jane Austen continually assures us of Elinor's strong feelings, and Marianne's latent sense, the two sisters occupy extreme positions throughout most of the novel. Ostensibly the author's sympathy is with Elinor, but running counter to this is Jane Austen's obvious admiration (reflected in lively description and dialogue) for Marianne's vitality and candor. It is as if Jane Austen's own sensibility were all on the side of

Marianne, but her judgment had to decide for Elinor; perhaps the novel's uncertainty reflects that of its creator. *Sense and Sensibility* provides strong support for Frank O'Connor's theory that Jane Austen "was a woman afraid of the violence of her own emotions, who rode the nightmare and sometimes rode it on too tight a rein." [24] Like *Northanger Abbey, Sense and Sensibility* tries to evaluate the sympathetic imagination and the spontaneous "moral sense" it promotes. When Elinor points out the impropriety of Marianne's visit to Allenham in the company of Willoughby, Marianne protests:

> "I never spent a pleasanter morning in my life."
> "I am afraid," replied Elinor, "that the pleasantness of an employment does not always evince its propriety."
> "On the contrary, nothing can be a stronger proof of it, Elinor; for if there had been any real impropriety in what I did, I should have been sensible of it at the time, for we always know when we are acting wrong, and with such a conviction I could have had no pleasure." (68)

Behind the debate between Elinor and Marianne we glimpse Jane Austen's own concern with the conflicting claims of reason and imagination, social custom and the free spirit. Her experience told her that Elinor's judgment and Marianne's sympathy both need qualification, but her attempts at this qualification in *Sense and Sensibility* are often merely verbal: we do not see them acted out, and therefore do not believe them.

A good illustration of the dilemma which Jane Austen faces may be found in those passages that deal with landscapes and picturesque taste. The reactions of the characters always push toward extremes.

> "And how does dear, dear Norland look?" cried Marianne.
> "Dear, dear Norland," said Elinor, "probably looks much as

it always does at this time of year. The woods and walks thickly covered with dead leaves."

"Oh!" cried Marianne, "with what transporting sensations have I formerly seen them fall! How have I delighted, as I walked, to see them driven in showers about me by the wind! What feelings have they, the season, the air altogether inspired! Now there is no one to regard them. They are seen only as a nuisance, swept hastily off, and driven as much as possible from the sight."

"It is not every one," said Elinor, "who has your passion for dead leaves." (87-8)

The novel strikes no middle ground between Marianne's passion for "dead leaves" and Edward's tepid liking for "civilized" nature; although Elinor *tells* us that Edward is not defective in natural taste (just as Jane Austen tells us that Elinor has strong feelings) we see little to demonstrate this.

"I like a fine prospect, [said Edward] but not on picturesque principles. I do not like crooked, twisted, blasted trees. I admire them much more if they are tall, straight and flourishing. I do not like ruined, tattered cottages. I am not fond of nettles, or thistles, or heath blossoms. I have more pleasure in a snug farm-house than a watch-tower—and a troop of tidy, happy villagers please me better than the finest banditti in the world." (98)

A comparison between these stock reactions and Elizabeth Bennet's appreciation of Pemberley underlines the difference between mechanical and creative uses of convention.

The unrealistic "type" characters of *Sense and Sensibility* are another indication of the novel's fundamental ambiguity. Willoughby appears to Marianne as the "hero of a favourite story" (43), and we are reminded of the "Quixotic" formula of the *Juvenilia,* in which the heroine's imaginative expectations (based on the "land of fiction") are shown to be false through exaggeration and broad irony. But in the burlesque *Juvenilia* there was no need for realism, whereas *Sense and Sensibility*—like any serious novel—is committed to the probable, and suffers from the fact that Willoughby remains for us as for Marianne a figure out of fiction. In *Sense and Sensibility* Jane Austen has moved beyond the world of burlesque, but she has not yet reached the stage where she can measure her characters' illusions against a sustained pattern of probable human behavior. Some of the novel's successes are of a kind familiar to us from the earlier works; others point forward to the subtleties of *Pride and Prejudice* or *Emma;* yet they are not parts of a unified drama, and they remain in our minds as isolated scenes. The novel threatens at every turn to resolve itself into unrealistic antitheses, and we must finally conclude that in providing Marianne with a choice between Willoughby's weakness and Colonel Brandon's "flannel waistcoat" Jane Austen was confessing her inability to transform the conventions inherited from other writers and embodied in the novel's original versions. Elinor's cautious decorum and occasional social hypocrisies scarcely make a valid alternative to the life of unrestrained feeling.

Marvin Mudrick has advanced the theory that Jane Austen, having abandoned the ironic attacks on excessive sensibility found in the *Juvenilia*, resorted in *Sense and Sensibility* to the self-defeating device of smothering feeling under dead social conventions. He makes the shrewd observations that Elinor, for all her Sense, has hardly been a better judge of Willoughby's character than Marianne; that her prudence is really a shrinking from commitment; and that Jane Austen's final exaltation of Elinor's judgment over Marianne's feeling is a falsification of the novel's action. Having demonstrated that the events of the novel do not confirm its ostensible theme, the

superiority of Sense to Sensibility, Mudrick then concludes
that in *Sense and Sensibility* Jane Austen turned from her
youthful attacks on false sensibility to an attack on all feeling.
"Feeling is bad because it is a personal commitment," and Jane
Austen, trapped in a world where the only alternative to
Willoughby is Colonel Brandon, finds her only solace in detachment. She defends herself against this world not with
irony, as in the earlier works, but with the lifeless façade of
socially accepted attitudes.[25]

This is in many ways a tempting view, but I cannot square
it with the general pattern of Jane Austen's development or
with the obvious attempts in *Sense and Sensibility* to mediate
between reason and feeling, social conventions and individual
passion. The alternative to Willoughby is Colonel Brandon
not because this was Jane Austen's heritage from life, but because it was her heritage from the broad antitheses of moralistic fiction. Similarly, Marianne's sensibility is continually de-
generating into excess, and Elinor's common-sense into lifeless
decorum, because it was the nature of the contemporary
novel's form and language to sharpen, rather than lessen, antitheses. Jane Austen's lack of enthusiasm for these schematic
oppositions is evident in the hackneyed tale with which Colonel Brandon explains Willoughby's character. The sincerity
and passion of Willoughby's final confession to Elinor indicate
the direction of the author's ambitions, but this fine scene is
ultimately negated by the reversion to literary stereotypes in
the final chapter.

The depressing atmosphere which hangs over so much of
Sense and Sensibility can, in short, be attributed to the fact
that Jane Austen was working against her natural inclinations
and talents. She was the victim of conventions, but these were
primarily artistic, not social. The brilliant ironic effects of her
earlier fiction had been local ones, and she was not able in her
revisions of *Sense and Sensibility* to evolve a structure that

could sustain her ironic vision. It was only with *Pride and Prejudice,* where the revisions struck much deeper, that she put her criticism of contemporary fiction to full use and achieved a form that we recognize as uniquely her own.

III

INTO THE
NINETEENTH CENTURY

The Watsons and *Pride and Prejudice*

The manuscript fragment known as *The Watsons* must have been begun soon after the sale of *Susan* (later *Northanger Abbey*) in the spring of 1803, and it seems likely that the story was broken off when Jane Austen realized that the publishers had no intention of bringing out *Susan*.[1] The natural disappointment caused by this failure (the novel had been advertised as "in the press"), combined with the unhappy circumstances of Jane Austen's life at the time, is sufficient to account for the fragment's being left unfinished. There are no inherent reasons of form and theme, as with *Lady Susan,* to explain her abandoning the work, and the intended developments recorded by the author of the *Memoir* seem both probable and promising.[2] We must assume that either personal distress or professional disappointment, most likely a combination of the two, caused Jane Austen to abandon the project. Perhaps the disasters of 1805–06—her father's death, a disorganized family life, the growing certainty that *Susan* would not appear—were directly responsible. But whatever the reasons for abandonment, and in spite of the work's unfinished nature and strained style, *The Watsons* marks a turning-point in Jane Austen's artistic development, and deserves more attention than has usually been accorded to it.

It is one of the signs of the unpropitious conditions under which the work was drafted that Jane Austen has lost interest in the ironic methods so brilliantly displayed in her earlier works. I believe Marvin Mudrick is right in claiming that the irony of *The Watsons* is "perfunctory" and almost reflexive, and that Jane Austen fails to exploit the situations which invite satire.[3] Even her criticism of Tom Musgrave, although consistently ironic, lacks intensity and acuteness. This shying-away from irony as a defining technique is part of what Mary Lascelles calls the "peculiar oppression" under which Jane Austen appears to be struggling, an oppression which is reflected in the "stiffness and heaviness that threaten her style,"[4] and which may have carried over into the last-minute revisions of *Sense and Sensibility*. But once this "peculiar oppression" is recognized and acknowledged, we do not need to accept Mudrick's theory that it stems from Jane Austen's first venture "in the grim business of vindicating genteel morality against the very society it is organized to uphold," and that she is "so pledged to her moral issue that she has lost any sustained shaping interest" in character and action.[5] Mudrick sees the center of the work as a conflict between a husband-hunting, mercenary society on the one hand, and a Sunday school morality on the other. In short, he sees *The Watsons* as a dress rehearsal for the triumph of genteel imperatives dramatized in *Mansfield Park*.

Behind this criticism of *The Watsons* lies the assumption that Jane Austen's characteristic (and only valid) artistic vision was marked by an aloof and defiant irony, and that her frequent retreats from this position represent artistic apostasies. Such a view strikes me as totally unacceptable, since it seizes upon only one of many qualities in her early work and labels that quality "characteristic," condemning all attempts at synthesis and accommodation as momentary lapses of artistic integrity under the pressure of moral and social conformity. If we read *The Watsons*—and later *Mansfield Park*—with the assumption that any departure from the impersonal irony of *Lady Susan* is an artistic apostasy, then we are bound to misread them. And if we approach the other novels in the same fashion, the distortion will be almost as great. Jane Austen's great strength lay in the complexity, the multiplicity, of her ways of seeing and expressing; the novels must be measured against each other and read in relation to her total achievement, not judged by a formula derived from a selective reading of her letters and a concentration on one aspect of her artistic power. If we are to understand *The Watsons* we must see it not as a foil to *Lady Susan* or a grim harbinger of gentility, but as a crucial stage in Jane Austen's artistic development, our only trustworthy guide to the nature and direction of her interests in the transitional period between the completion of *Northanger Abbey* and the last-minute revisions of *Sense and Sensibility*.

In *The Watsons* Jane Austen, a spinster nearing thirty who had probably relinquished all hopes of an equal marriage, squarely confronted her major theme: the conflict between the free spirit and social-economic imperatives. It was a great theme ideally suited to the narrow world of her observation, since in the struggle for marriage and security she found a perfect figure for the general plight of the free spirit. In the first versions of *Sense and Sensibility* she had already explored the limitations of two positions, that in which the individual claims greater freedom than he actually possesses (Marianne's independence) and that in which the individual, through extreme prudence and a fear of engagement, limits himself beyond the natural restrictions of birth and environment (this would be Elinor). In the first version of *Pride and Prejudice* —and we can only guess at its form—Elizabeth and Darcy may have played similar roles, and their marriage may have represented, as it does in the final version, an ideal accommodation, although one which Jane Austen could never repeat. In these works the play of opposites was dramatized in opposed characters, sisters or lovers, but in *The Watsons* Jane Austen attempted for the first time to present her subject not through paired characters (as with Catherine Morland and Henry Tilney) but through the mind of her central figure. In this the fragment looks forward to *Emma* and *Persuasion*, just as its characters and situations point forward to the fiction of the 1811–17 period.[6] Emma Watson is deliberately pictured as an isolated and sensitive person, cut off from all expectations and trapped in an alien world, who must make her way as she can. Her situation is an epitome of the dilemma faced by the free spirit in a limited world, and—in so far as we can tell from the fragment—it was part of Jane Austen's purpose to present her without confidante or counterpart.

In this isolation of the heroine, with all its tragic implications, *The Watsons* seems closer to *Mansfield Park, Emma,* and *Persuasion* than to *Pride and Prejudice;* for although *Pride and Prejudice* must have undergone extensive revision in 1811–12, its scaffolding of characters and situations harks back to the 1790's, while *The Watsons* was conceived in the barren middle period of Jane Austen's career. The social world of *The Watsons* seems more "modern" than that of *Pride and Prejudice,* and is two generations removed from the society of *Lady Susan.* While *Lady Susan* focuses on the same society as Fanny Burney's *Evelina* (1778), *The Watsons* belongs to the nineteenth century, and in many ways seems closer to the world of Mrs. Gaskell than to that of Fanny Burney. It presents the plight of impoverished gentility in a society where the old economic relationships are breaking down. Robert

Watson represents one extreme of the new bourgeois pros-
perity (just as Elizabeth Bennet's aunt and uncle, the Gardiners, represent another extreme), and in her treatment of
him Jane Austen reveals her determination to follow the
course of contemporary manners. Indeed, the most striking
quality of *The Watsons* is its departure from the ideological
frame of *Sense and Sensibility*. Any census of the vocabulary
of judgment in *Sense and Sensibility* and *The Watsons* will
reveal a striking disparity: words such as Understanding,
Sensibility, Wit, Imagination are used sparingly in the latter
work—more sparingly than in *Pride and Prejudice*—and Jane
Austen seems completely absorbed in the dramatic rendering
of contemporary manners. Ten years later, in a letter criticizing the fiction of her niece Anna, Jane Austen laid great
stress on a first-hand knowledge of manners: "Let the Port-
mans go to Ireland, but as you know nothing of the Manners
there, you had better not go with them." [7] It is clear that by
"Manners" Jane Austen does not mean just the protocols of
society, although she demanded a faithful rendering of these
("A Country Surgeon . . . would not be introduced to Men
of their rank" [8]) and understood that their significance
stretched beyond mere verisimilitude. To her, at least in her
later novels, "Manners" takes on the rich significance discussed by Lionel Trilling in his essay on "Manners, Morals
and the Novel":

> What I understand by manners, then, is a culture's hum and
> buzz of implication. I mean the whole evanescent context in
> which its explicit statements are made. It is that part of a cul-
> ture which is made up of half-uttered or unuttered or unutter-
> able expressions of value. They are hinted at by small actions,
> sometimes by the arts of dress or decoration, sometimes by tone,
> gesture, emphasis, or rhythm, sometimes by the words that are
> used with a special frequency or a special meaning. [9]

In the more serious *Juvenilia,* in *Sense and Sensibility,* and in *Northanger Abbey* we can trace a gradual flowering of Jane Austen's notion of manners and the uses to which they can be put in fiction. But in all these works her characters, no matter how animated, are blends of observation and literary reminiscence. They belong to the contemporary literary world, cleared of the rubbish attacked in the *Juvenilia,* and the movements they make in the novels' development are partially dictated by an inherited ideological pattern. But in *The Watsons* Jane Austen broke away from the limits of eighteenth-century themes, and allowed the manners of the world around her to direct the novel's growth. In discarding the sturdy supports of eighteenth-century antitheses she found herself in possession of materials not yet assimilated by fiction, and these demanded new techniques and devices. In *The Watsons* Jane Austen is straining after methods of organization and presentation adequate to her developing grasp of manners, and this strain may account in some measure for the work's stiffness, and perhaps for its final rejection or abandonment.

In *The Watsons* Jane Austen is so intent on the social discriminations she is making that, for once, she fails to give us a double vision of her heroine. Her view is completely coincident with that of Emma Watson, and although later revisions might have introduced a qualifying irony, the fragment as it stands is unique in Jane Austen's achievement. Emma is subject to none of the misapprehensions and self-deceptions of the other heroines; instead she is a passive center, reminding one of the passive observers in Henry James's work of the 1890's, and all her efforts are aimed at comprehension of a new environment. Jane Austen is, it would appear, deliberately eschewing direct judgment as she works her way into the situation; instead there is an attempt to cast everything in dramatic form, to embody as much of the judgment as possible in dialogue and action. In short, *The Watsons* throws a great deal of responsibility for judgment on the reader, who must follow Jane Austen's indirections and construct his own view of the relationships between the characters. The opening pages of the tale contain less "historical" commentary by the author than those of any other work, and the entire burden of exposition is placed on dialogue. Instead of describing Emma and Elizabeth, Jane Austen allows their characters to emerge from the long dialogue between the sisters. As Elizabeth sketches in the family situation we are faced with the problem of qualifying her statements in the light of her character and personal involvement, and Jane Austen does little to help us here. The greatest technical departure of *The Watsons* over Jane Austen's previous fiction lies in this reliance on the dramatic method, and we may surmise that her withdrawal from the story was prompted in large measure by dissatisfaction with the conflicts between dramatic implication and authorial comment which had often cropped up in her earlier fiction. She had not yet learned to blend the two into an organized and unified whole.

The skill with which Jane Austen could command the techniques of a dramatic scene is revealed at the Ball, where Tom Musgrave's parasitic actions, and Emma's unaffected concern for Charles Blake's disappointment, are epiphanies of character. The entire scene is a model of economy. As the party from Osborne Castle enter they are described with few details, so that we know no more of their respective natures than does Emma; indeed, we see their entrance as if through her eyes.

> Emma looked at them all as they passed—but chiefly & with most interest on Tom Musgrave, who was certainly a genteel, good looking young man.—Of the females, Ly. Osborne had by much the finest person;—tho' nearly 50, she was very handsome, & had all the Dignity of Rank.—
>
> Ld Osborne was a very fine young man; but there was an air

of Coldness, of Carelessness, even of Awkwardness about him, which seemed to speak him out of his Element in a Ball room. He came in fact only because it was judged expedient for him to please the Borough—he was not fond of Women's company, & he never danced.—Mr Howard was an agreable-looking Man, a little more than Thirty.— (329–30)

Yet from these spare beginnings the scene builds up to a substantial revelation of character, and this revelation is accomplished through dialogue and action. Miss Osborne's light dismissal of her promise to Charles, Tom Musgrave's position as an errand-boy for Lord Osborne, the awkward attentions of Lord Osborne himself, and Emma's own open nature—all are clearly presented, and with a minimum of authorial intrusion. It is only in the final passage of the fragment, when Jane Austen's interest flags, that we return to simple exposition:

> In *his* chamber, Emma was at peace from the dreadful mortifications of unequal Society, & family Discord—from the immediate endurance of Hard-hearted prosperity, low-minded Conceit, & wrong-headed folly, engrafted on an untoward Disposition. She still suffered from them in the Contemplation of their existence; in memory & in prospect, but for the moment, she ceased to be tortured by their effects.—She was at leisure, she could read & think,—tho' her situation was hardly such as to make reflection very soothing. The Evils arising from the loss of her Uncle, were neither trifling, nor likely to lessen; & when Thought had been freely indulged, in contrasting the past & the present, the employment of mind, the dissipation of unpleasant ideas which only reading could produce, made her thankfully turn to a book. (361)

The contrast between this lifeless prose and the energy of the ball-room scene leaves little doubt as to the future direction of Jane Austen's artistic development. Although she would return in later works to a steady management of external comment, and would never again entrust so great a burden to dramatic scene and unqualified observation, the need for a more flexible blending of internal and external methods had been recognized. Her growing awareness of the richness and complexity of manners demanded new methods of expression.

The unfinished nature of *The Watsons* is vexatious, but it is not without its compensations, since the manuscript provides us with detailed evidence of Jane Austen's methods of composition. We know from her letters to Anna Austen that Jane was devoted to careful revision, and in a letter to Cassandra concerning *Pride and Prejudice* she refers to the novel as having been "lop't and crop't." [10] *The Watsons* furnishes our only clear evidence of her working methods during the first half of her career: the changes in the *Juvenilia* are too scrappy to be of much use, and the other manuscripts (*Sanditon* and the canceled chapter of *Persuasion*) belong to the period 1816–17. The manuscript of *The Watsons* is copiously corrected, and this perplexity may have resulted in part from the artistic and personal uncertainties which surrounded its composition; but we must assume that even at the height of her artistic assurance Jane Austen subjected her works to searching revisions. The manuscript of *The Watsons* displays at some points three or more separate stages of revision, and presumably it would have been subjected to several more reworkings before publication.

Although it is hard to generalize on the changes in *The Watsons,* we can say that most of them square with the principles of selection and construction which Jane Austen recommended to her niece Anna.[11] Most of the revisions are small verbal alterations, modifications of a word, phrase, or sentence. The effect of any one change seems almost negligible, but the cumulative effect can hardly be overemphasized. As Mary Lascelles has pointed out, it seems to have been Jane Austen's custom to sketch out "first what her characters have to communicate," and then to mark, "by gradual little touches, the manner of communication." [12] In the revisions she gradually builds up the distinguishing idioms of her characters, emphasizing their idiosyncrasies and sharpening the dramatic differences. Thus in Elizabeth's description of Tom Musgrave, "philandering" is replaced by "behaving in a particular way"; and in her description of Margaret, "has a good deal of spirit" gives way to "is a little fretful & perverse." [13] In both cases the revisions are closer to Elizabeth's characteristic speech, and more revealing of her attitudes toward the other characters. Similarly, Musgrave's gratitude at being admitted "in such a state into your Drawing room" is altered to "in such Dishabille," emphasizing his false elegance.[14]

There are other modes of revision which remind us of the advice to Anna. In reworking the description of Mr. Edward's house Jane Austen excised several details, among them the color of the house ("dull brick") and the number and color of the posts that guard the door.[15] By paring down this description she was following her customary policy of keeping extraneous details to a minimum: "your descriptions are often more minute than will be liked," she wrote to Anna. "You give too many particulars of right hand & left." [16] But parallel to this sparing use of descriptive detail ran a passion for minute accuracy in geography and chronology, reflected in *The Watsons* by various changes in the names of towns and by a tidying-up of the chronology (Emma's absence from home is finally fixed at fourteen years). Evidently Jane Austen felt an acute need for some grounding in realistic detail, as in her use of almanacs and roadbooks when constructing her later novels.[17] Throughout her letters to Anna she displays a persistent concern for accuracy of detail; as R. W. Chapman has said, she "knows all the details, and gives us very few of them." [18] The important thing was not the reader's awareness of this consistency in detail, but her own secure knowledge of it. Like James Joyce after her, Jane Austen found in accuracy of setting an essential underpinning for the deeper psychological realism of her fiction.

Other characteristics of the revisions are a tendency to recast narrative statements in dramatic form, and a desire to reduce extended speeches to fast-paced dialogue. Thus Margaret's original response to Tom Musgrave's praise of Miss Osborne's beauty—"She is about as fair as I am, I think"—becomes "Is she fairer than me?," to which Musgrave makes no reply.[19] Or again, the author's statement, "But to this Emma could not quite agree . . . ," is replaced by a bit of dialogue: "No, no, said Emma laughing you must sit with my friends." [20] Similarly, Mary Edward's account of her companions at the Ball, "Mr Norton is a Cousin of Capt. Hunter's & Mr Styles is one of his particular freinds," is sharpened by the insertion of a question from her father: "Mr Norton is a Cousin of Capt. Hunter's."— "And who is Mr Styles?" "One of his particular friends." [21]

In general, the revision of the dialogue moves toward a more realistic give-and-take, and away from the set speeches so common in Jane Austen's earlier works. This can be seen in a short passage of dialogue which was added in the course of revision. In the original draft the decision to play Vingt-un was followed immediately by a description of Tom Musgrave's lively direction of the game, but later Jane Austen inserted the following:

> "Do you see much of the Parsonage family at the Castle, Mr Musgrave?—" said Emma, as they were taking their seats.—"Oh! yes—they are almost always there. Mrs Blake is a nice little good-humoured Woman, she & I are sworn friends; & Howard's a very gentlemanlike good sort of fellow!—You are not forgotten I assure you by any of the party. I fancy you must have a little cheek-glowing now & then Miss Emma. Were not you rather warm last Saturday about 9 or 10 o'clock in the Even^g—? I will

tell you how it was.—I see you are dieing to know.—Says Howard to Ld Osborne—" At this interesting moment he was called
on by the others, to regulate the game & determine some dis-
putable point; & his attention was so totally engaged in the
business & afterwards by the course of the game as never to revert to what he had been saying before;—& Emma, tho' suffering a good deal from Curiosity, dared not remind him.[22]

Apparently Jane Austen felt that by adding some hint of
Emma's interest in Mr. Howard she could prevent the reader
from transferring his full attention to the subsidiary Margaret-
Musgrave plot.

The various motives for revision are found together in the
development of one complex passage. During the visit of Musgrave and Lord Osborne to the Watsons' home the conversation turns to horseback riding, and Lord Osborne remarks that
"A woman never looks better than on horseback." Emma reminds him that "every woman may not have the inclination,
or the means," to which Lord Osborne replies:

"If they knew how much it became them, they would all have
the inclination, & I fancy Miss Watson—when once they had
the inclination, the means w^d soon follow." (345–6)

In the earliest draft this broad hint at Lord Osborne's feeling
for Emma was followed by the passage below (all phrases in
brackets were inserted above the lines).

"You mean [I am to suppose] a compliment of course my
Lord, said Emma bowing, tho' I do [can] not exactly understand [define] it." Lord Osborne laughed rather awkwardly—
& then said "Upon my soul, I am a bad one for Compliments.
Nobody can be a worse hand at it [such things] than myself."
[I wish I knew more of the matter] and after some minutes
silence—added, "Can [not] you give me a lesson Miss Watson
on the art of paying Comp^ts—I should be very glad to learn." I

want very much to know how to please the Ladies—one Lady at
least [A cold monosyllable & grave look from Emma repressed
the growing] freedom of his manner. He had too much sence,
not to take the hint—& when he spoke again, it was with a degree of courteous propriety which he had never used before.
[was not often at] the trouble of using [employing.] [23]

But this expression of Emma's bewilderment, and the subsequent broadening of the hint, could not be reconciled with
Jane Austen's developing sense of Lord Osborne's character
and Emma's perceptivity. It was completely canceled, and
replaced by a more subtle exchange:

"Your Lordship thinks we always have our own way.—*That*
is a point on which Ladies & Gentle^n have long disagreed—But
without pretending to decide it, I may say that there are some
circumstances which even *Women* cannot controul.—Female
Economy may do a great deal, but it cannot turn a small income
into a large one."—Ld Osborne was silenced. Her manner had
been neither sententious nor sarcastic, but there was a something in what she said which made his Lordship think;—and
when he addressed her again, it was with courteous propriety,
totally unlike the half-awkward, half-fearless stile of his former
remarks.—It was a new thing with him to wish to please a
woman; it was the first time that he had ever felt what was due
to a woman his equal in Education.—But as he wanted neither
Sense nor a good disposition, he did not feel it without resolv-
ing on the necessary effort.—"You have not been long in this
Country I understand, said he. I hope you are pleased with
it." [24]

This passage is more in keeping with our impression of
Emma's social awareness, and it does justice to Lord Osborne's
personality. Instead of a brash suggestion suppressed by a
"cold monosyllable & grave look" we have Emma directing the
conversation in a manner "neither sententious nor sarcastic"

which evokes Lord Osborne's native tact. The second version is a great improvement over the first in psychological terms, but it still did not satisfy Jane Austen's ear, and in a subsequent revision several small changes were made. Emma's speech was rendered more natural, and the uninformative "something in what she said" was altered to: "something in it's mild seriousness, as well as in the words themselves." Lord Osborne's "courteous propriety" was replaced by "a degree of considerate propriety," and the reference to Emma as "a woman his equal in Education" gave way to the more comprehensive "a woman, in Emma's situation," which includes her impoverished and dependent status as well as her genteel background. All these changes and expansions were carried out in the interest of exactly defining the relationship between Lord Osborne and Emma. Behind the revisions of *The Watsons* we glimpse an unrealized ideal, the ideal of a fictional form in which every detail of description or dialogue is part of a graceful and unified design.

With *Pride and Prejudice* Jane Austen bid farewell to her early life and to the eighteenth century. We have seen that the recasting of *Sense and Sensibility* in 1809–11 never reached the vital centers of that novel; the original antitheses and conventions protrude through the final structure. But the late revisions of *Pride and Prejudice* (c. 1811–12) were so elaborate, and penetrated so deeply into the novel's language and action, that they amounted to a re-seeing of the entire work. Although it is impossible to reconstruct the details of *First Impressions*, we can say with some assurance that the finished novel was far removed from this early draft. Ten days after the publication of *Pride and Prejudice* Jane Austen wrote to Cassandra: "I am exceedingly pleased that you can say what you do, after having gone thro' the whole work." [25] This remark, as Mary Lascelles has pointed out, suggests a substantial difference between *First Impressions* and the published novel, since Jane Austen would have long been familiar with Cassandra's opinions of the early version.[26] Another indication of the extent of the revisions may be found in the elaborate use of the 1811–12 almanacs; the consistency of the novel's time-scheme could only have resulted from a thorough reworking of the plot.[27] But more important than this historical evidence is the general evidence of the novel's style, which is more uniform and sophisticated than that of *Sense and Sensibility*. In recasting *Sense and Sensibility* Jane Austen was doing the best job she could with a work already moribund in her imagination. But *Pride and Prejudice* remained alive for her, its hero and heroine perpetually interesting.[28] On 24 May 1813, after a visit to "the Exhibition in Spring Gardens" held by the Society of Painters in Oil and Water Colours, she wrote to Cassandra:

> It is not thought a good collection, but I was very well pleased —particularly (pray tell Fanny) with a small portrait of Mrs. Bingley, excessively like her. I went in hopes of seeing one of her Sister, but there was no Mrs. Darcy;—perhaps however, I may find her in the Great Exhibition which we shall go to, if we have time . . . Mrs. Bingley's is exactly herself, size, shaped face, features & sweetness; there never was a greater likeness. She is dressed in a white gown, with green ornaments, which convinces me of what I had always supposed, that green was a favourite colour with her. I dare say Mrs. D. will be in Yellow.

And later in the same letter:

> We have been both to the Exhibition & Sir J. Reynolds',—and I am disappointed, for there was nothing like Mrs. D. at either. I can only imagine that Mr. D. prizes any Picture of her too much to like it should be exposed to the public eye.—I can

imagine he w^d have that sort of feeling—that mixture of Love, Pride & Delicacy.[29]

It would seem that *Pride and Prejudice* remained fresh and exciting in Jane Austen's imagination for two reasons: first, the charm of the heroine, "as delightful a creature as ever appeared in print"; [30] and second, her pleasure in having successfully reformed the original story to accord with her new ideals in theme and technique. We cannot think of *Pride and Prejudice* as belonging to any one period of Jane Austen's life before 1813; rather it was a summing up of her artistic career, a valedictory to the world of *Sense and Sensibility* and a token of things to come. More than any other of her novels it deserves Henry Austen's description in his Biographical Notice: "Some of these novels had been the gradual performances of her previous life." [31]

One index to the new tones and new attitudes struck in *Pride and Prejudice* is the novel's use of conventions and stock situations drawn from eighteenth-century fiction. Both *Sense and Sensibility* and *Pride and Prejudice* depend upon characters and actions inherited from the Richardson-Fanny Burney tradition: the attractive seducer, the thoughtless young hoyden, ill-mannered relatives, tyrannical aristocrats, elopements and assignations. It is obvious from the *Juvenilia* that Jane Austen recognized the potential absurdity of these conventions; but they were so much a part of her fictional experience, and in some cases so close to the actual world she knew, that she could not exclude them from her art. The superiority of *Pride and Prejudice* to *Sense and Sensibility* lies in the transformation of these stale conventions, which renders them a believable part of the action and a natural vehicle for the novel's themes. This difference may be seen in a comparison of the heroes and villains, Darcy with Colonel Brandon, Wickham with Willoughby. In *Sense and Sensibility* Colonel Bran-

don has no more life than Lord Orville in Fanny Burney's
Evelina; we believe in what he represents, but not in him. Yet
Darcy, while preserving the virtues of the fictional hero, is
entirely believable, since Jane Austen has subjected him to a
process of self-evaluation and self-recognition. In him the type
has been revivified. Similarly, the story of Willoughby's past
behavior (as told by Colonel Brandon) is merely a plot device,
a tale of seduction borrowed from fiction in the hope that it
will give Willoughby's villainy substance and shape. In fact
the tale stamps Willoughby as a two-dimensional figure; it sub-
stitutes his prototype in *Evelina* for the man we have glimpsed
earlier, and not even the moving final confession can re-
assert his reality. But in *Pride and Prejudice* Wickham, although a descendant of the eighteenth-century fictional rake,
does not suffer from the defects of his originals: his elopement
with Lydia is plausible and carefully prepared, not a stale convention dragged in to forward the plot; and Darcy's account
of Wickham's past villainies, unlike Colonel Brandon's tale,
seems consonant with all we know of the subject's character.

It is important to keep these distinctions between *Sense
and Sensibility* and *Pride and Prejudice* in mind when we
speak of the latter's origins in late eighteenth-century fiction.
Jane Austen's admiration of Fanny Burney is well known,
and there can be no doubt that *Pride and Prejudice*—or, more
exactly, *First Impressions*—owed a debt to *Cecilia*.[32] Q. D.
Leavis exaggerates this debt in her statement that "the original conception of *First Impressions* was undoubtedly to re-
write the story of Cecilia in realistic terms," [33] but we know
that when Jane Austen began work on the story the world of
Evelina and *Cecilia* held a great reality for her. A niece recol-
lected hearing, as a very young child, Jane Austen "read a part
out of *Evelina,* one of the chapters concerning the Branghtons
and Mr. Smith, and she thought it sounded like a play." [34]
Fanny Burney's fiction is filled with figures who remind us of

Colonel Brandon or Willoughby or Lydia or Mrs. Bennet, and although one can argue that these were common types, the details of their treatment in Jane Austen's early work are often reminiscent of Fanny Burney. More significantly, the struggle between personal affection and family pride in *Cecilia* may have suggested the major themes of *Pride and Prejudice;* certainly the title was taken from the conclusion to *Cecilia,* where Dr. Lyster points the story's moral.

"The whole of this unfortunate business . . . has been the result of PRIDE and PREJUDICE. . . . Yet this, however, remember; if to PRIDE and PREJUDICE you owe your miseries, so wonderfully is good and evil balanced, that to PRIDE and PREJUDICE you will also owe their termination."

But these similarities between *Pride and Prejudice* and Fanny Burney's novels only intensify our sense of Jane Austen's achievement in transforming the conventions of "the land of fiction." Since the limited social world she observed had been the subject of so much previous fiction, she was prevented from seeking originality in new situations and new locales. Instead she had to find her voice within the same range of life explored by many other female writers. Bingley's arrival at Netherfield, the ballroom scene, Wickham's flirtations, Darcy's letter, Lydia's elopement, Lady Catherine's condescending visit—these were standard raw materials, but in *Pride and Prejudice* they were endowed with such a quantity of "felt life," and incorporated so skillfully into the drama, that they took on a new significance. It is this transformation of familiar materials which yields one of the novel's chief pleasures, the sense of subtle variations within a fixed and traditional range of experience. *Pride and Prejudice* bears that hallmark of "classic" art, the discovery of new possibilities within a traditional form.

Although the phrase "Pride and Prejudice" does not suggest as neat an ideological antithesis as "Sense and Sensibility," it would have led a late eighteenth-century reader to expect a schematic drama in which each quality is represented by a separate character or faction. But in *Pride and Prejudice* one cannot equate Darcy with Pride, or Elizabeth with Prejudice; Darcy's pride of place is founded on social prejudice, while Elizabeth's initial prejudice against him is rooted in pride of her own quick perceptions. In this we have a clear indication of the novel's distance from *Cecilia*, for Jane Austen's "internalizing" of the conflicts between proper and improper pride, candor and prejudice, goes far beyond the capabilities of Fanny Burney. Indeed, it was this ability to vest the novel's conflicts in the dynamic development of personality that freed Jane Austen from the world of static values which still dominates in *Sense and Sensibility*. Whereas in *Sense and Sensibility* the antitheses are resolved by a suppression of one position and an uneasy exaltation of the other, the entire movement of *Pride and Prejudice* tends toward a resolution of conflicts which is a union rather than a compromise, a union in which both parties gain new vigor and freedom of expression. The marriage of Elizabeth and Darcy resolves not only their personal differences but the conflicts they have represented, with the result that the novel provides a final pleasure unique in Jane Austen's fiction, a sense of complete fulfillment analogous to that which marks the end of some musical compositions. It is this sense of a union of opposites—without injury to the identity of either—which prompts the common comparison with Mozart. In *Pride and Prejudice*, for once in her career, Jane Austen allowed the symmetry of her imaginative creation to prevail over the protests of her social self, and the result is a triumph of ideal form. It was a triumph not to be repeated, one that was replaced in the later novels by less comforting views of human nature. Yet it remains valid as the finest expression of one aspect of Jane Austen's personality, her desire to endow human behavior with the order and symmetry of art. *Pride and Prejudice* is a great comedy because it formulates an ideal vision of human possibilities; its ending is "realistic" not because we measure the union of Elizabeth and Darcy against our own experience (that experience which delights in Jane Austen's statement that Mrs. Bennet remained "occasionally nervous and invariably silly"), but because their marriage is a complete fulfillment of the novel's artistic imperatives. Their lives have been the work's structure, and their marriage is a vindication of the artist's power to resolve complexities.

In his penetrating essay on *Mansfield Park* Lionel Trilling defines the special quality that distinguishes *Pride and Prejudice* from Jane Austen's other works.

> The great charm, the charming greatness, of *Pride and Prejudice* is that it permits us to conceive of morality as style. The relation of Elizabeth Bennet to Darcy is real, is intense, but it expresses itself as a conflict and reconciliation of styles: a formal rhetoric, traditional and rigorous, must find a way to accommodate a female vivacity, which in turn must recognize the principled demands of the strict male syntax. The high moral import of the novel lies in the fact that the union of styles is accomplished without injury to either lover.[35]

Pride and Prejudice does more than testify to the artist's capacity for organizing and clarifying the confusions of life; it supports the fine illusion that life itself can take on the discrimination and selectivity of art. Throughout the novel aesthetic and moral values are closely related. Darcy and Elizabeth share the common eighteenth-century assumption that a man of real taste is usually a man of sound moral judgment,[36] and when Elizabeth first views Pemberley the tasteful prospect confirms her altered opinion of Darcy's character:

> Elizabeth's mind was too full for conversation, but she saw and admired every remarkable spot and point of view. They gradually ascended for half a mile, and then found themselves at the top of a considerable eminence, where the wood ceased, and the eye was instantly caught by Pemberley House, situated on the opposite side of a valley, into which the road with some abruptness wound. It was a large, handsome, stone building, standing well on rising ground, and backed by a ridge of high woody hills;—and in front, a stream of some natural importance was swelled into greater, but without any artificial appearance. Its banks were neither formal, nor falsely adorned. Elizabeth was delighted. She had never seen a place for which nature had done more, or where natural beauty had been so little counteracted by an awkward taste. They were all of them warm in their admiration; and at that moment she felt, that to be mistress of Pemberley might be something! (245)

Every evidence of sound aesthetic judgment provided by Pemberley is converted by Elizabeth into evidence of Darcy's natural amiability, and joined with the enthusiastic testimony of the housekeeper, until Pemberley becomes an image of his true nature. Sir Walter Scott was not entirely imperceptive when he made his much-ridiculed remark that Elizabeth "does not perceive that she has done a foolish thing until she accidentally visits a very handsome seat and grounds belonging to her admirer." [37] Pemberley is more than a reminder of lost social and economic possibilities; it is a solid reflection of Elizabeth's new attitude toward Darcy.

This close connection between aesthetic and moral judgments enables Jane Austen to express her moral themes in terms of the novel's movement from complex antitheses to easy resolution. As Darcy and Elizabeth are first presented to us they sum up most of the conflicting forces in Jane Austen's early fiction. Elizabeth possesses the illusion of total freedom; she looks to nature, rather than society or traditional authority, for the basis of her judgments. She is self-reliant and proud of her discernment, contemptuous of all conventions that constrict the individual's freedom. Darcy, on the other hand, is mindful of his relationship to society, proud of his social place, and aware of the restrictions that inevitably limit the free spirit. Together they dramatize the persistent conflict between social restraint and the individual will, between tradition and self-expression.

Both Darcy and Elizabeth are flanked by figures who parody their basic tendencies: in Mr. Bennet the irony of the detached observer has become sterile, while Lady Catherine de Bourgh represents the worst side of aristocratic self-consciousness. But it is another group that provides the full antidote to pride and prejudice. The Gardiners stand as a rebuke to Darcy's social prejudices and aristocratic pride, an example of natural aristocracy; while Wickham's true nature is a telling blow to Elizabeth's pride of perception, and to her prejudice in favor of "natural" goodness. The marriage of Elizabeth and Darcy is, as Mark Schorer has pointed out, a kind of economic and social merging, an accommodation of traditional values based upon status with the new values personified in the Gardiners.[38] Elizabeth is led to an appreciation of Darcy's "proper" pride—"he has no improper pride," she ultimately protests to Mr. Bennet (376)—while Darcy is disabused of his inherited prejudices based on caste and economic distance. But it would be too much to say, as Schorer does, that Jane Austen embodies her social judgments in Darcy, and her moral judgments in Elizabeth. For it is part of the novel's purpose to demonstrate that Elizabeth's original opinions were not freely arrived at, but conditioned by social prejudice, while Darcy's initial pride had its roots in a feeling of moral superiority. The first two volumes of *Pride and Prejudice* are so complex that no one set of antitheses can define the positions of the hero and heroine, and any attempt to establish rigid patterns leads to absurdity. Under such schematizing Darcy's ambivalent attitude is reduced to the pomposity of Mary's extracts, while Elizabeth's wit becomes as sterile as her father's.

During recent years several intelligent critics have analyzed the stylistic and dramatic techniques used by Jane Austen to mark the subtle changes in the relationship between Darcy and Elizabeth.[39] The most persuasive of these critics, Reuben Brower, has shown that all of the surface wit and irony of the novel is *functional*, a part of the larger dramatic design. Through a "sheer poetry of wit" Jane Austen conveys multiple views of her major characters, yet never does she lose sight of her fundamental dramatic aims. The greatness of the novel —whatever its limitations may be—lies in her fusion of the poetry of wit with the dramatic structure of fiction.[40] It is this combination of local complexity with a general clarity of design which animates the novel, and redeems a story which could have been as static as that of *Sense and Sensibility*. A perfect example of the organic connection between language and action may be found in the speeches of Elizabeth and Darcy, which change as the differences between them are reconciled. In the novel's early scenes Jane Austen establishes a clear-cut distinction between Elizabeth's lively speech and Darcy's formal language, but this difference in expressive style is gradually modified as each begins to appreciate the other's style of living. When Darcy learns of the changes in Elizabeth's feelings toward him he expresses himself "as sensibly and as warmly as a man violently in love can be supposed to do" (366), while Elizabeth's defense of her engagement to Mr. Bennet is reminiscent of Darcy's earlier remarks on the virtues of proper pride: "Indeed he has no improper pride. He is perfectly amiable" (376). In the conventional final chapter of *Pride and Prejudice*, where the future lives of the characters are confidently charted, Jane Austen can summarize with such easy authority because we have already seen these relationships foreshadowed in the novel's language and action.

The foundation of Jane Austen's success in correlating language and action is her irony, and the nature of this irony is nowhere better displayed than in the permutations of the novel's first sentence: "It is a truth universally acknowledged, that a single man in possession of a good fortune, must be in want of a wife." Out of context this general statement may seem no more significant than its original in *Rambler* No. 115, where Hymenaeus writes:

> "I was known to possess a fortune, and to want a wife; and therefore was frequently attended by those hymeneal solicitors, with whose importunity I was sometimes diverted, and sometimes perplexed; for they contended for me as vultures for a carcase; each employing all his eloquence, and all his artifices, to enforce and promote his own scheme, from the success of which he was to receive no other advantage than the pleasure of defeating others equally eager, and equally industrious."

Yet even in isolation the novel's opening sentence contains a certain irony: the exaggeration of the statement jars against our sense of reality, and prepares us for the discovery in the first chapters of *Pride and Prejudice* that this "truth" is acknowledged only by Mrs. Bennet and her kind. In the context of these chapters the irony is directed at economic motives for marriage, but as the action develops the implications of the opening sentence are modified and extended, until by the end of the novel we are willing to acknowledge that both Bingley and Darcy were "in want of a wife." Thus the sentence is simultaneously a source for irony and a flat statement of the social and personal necessities which dominate the world of *Pride and Prejudice*. The basic truth of the generalization is untouched by its ironic potential, and this suggests an important distinction that must be made in any discussion of Jane Austen's mature art. Her irony is dramatic, not static; complex, not simple; and we can only judge the tenor of the author's comments or the professions of her characters against the total pattern of dramatic action. Take for an example the following dialogue between Darcy and Elizabeth:

"What think you of books?" said he, smiling.

"Books—Oh! no.—I am sure we never read the same, or not with the same feelings."

"I am sorry you think so; but if that be the case, there can at least be no want of subject.—We may compare our different opinions."

"No—I cannot talk of books in a ball-room; my head is always full of something else."

"The *present* always occupies you in such scenes—does it?" said he, with a look of doubt.

"Yes, always," she replied, without knowing what she said, for her thoughts had wandered far from the subject, as soon afterwards appeared by her suddenly exclaiming, "I remember hearing you once say, Mr. Darcy, that you hardly ever forgave, that your resentment once created was unappeasable. You are very cautious, I suppose, as to its *being created*."

"I am," said he, with a firm voice.

"And never allow yourself to be blinded by prejudice?"

"I hope not."

"It is particularly incumbent on those who never change their opinion, to be secure of judging properly at first."

"May I ask to what these questions tend?"

"Merely to the illustration of *your* character," said she, endeavouring to shake off her gravity. "I am trying to make it out." (93)

By the time we have reached this passage in the novel we know enough of Darcy's nature, and Elizabeth's pride of judgment, to realize that the questions tend more to an illustration of *her* character than of his. In this exchange Jane Austen is depending on an immediate grasp of the inherent dramatic irony, and she has carefully prepared her audience by allowing them to see more of the truth of the situation than any one character can perceive. But a first encounter with this passage does not exhaust its ironic implications, and only in retrospect— or upon second reading—do we understand its relation to the total pattern of dramatic action. The point about such compli- cated irony is that it depends on a full *external* revelation of the characters' inner natures; we rely more upon what they say and do than upon the author's comments. In this passage, as in so many others, we are reminded of the novel's affinities with the best in eighteenth-century drama. The tripartite struc- ture of *Pride and Prejudice,* dictated by the conventional three-decker form of publication, is similar to the structure of a three-act play, and we know from a remark in one of her letters to Cassandra that Jane Austen considered the volumes as separate units:

> The second volume is shorter than I could wish, but the differ- ence is not so much in reality as in look, there being a larger proportion of narrative in that part.[41]

This remark reveals the dramatist's eye for symmetry, but the reference to "a larger proportion of narrative" is scarcely apolo- getic, and we must realize that Jane Austen's method in *Pride and Prejudice* depends heavily on scenic effects but is not lim- ited to them. The first half of the novel could easily be trans- lated into a play; here Darcy and Elizabeth are "on stage," joining with the other characters to dramatize the novel's psy- chological and social conflicts. Howard S. Babb has shown how Jane Austen plays on the word "performance" in the early dialogues, bringing all the implications of the word together in the great scene at Rosings (174–6), where Elizabeth's actual performance at the piano becomes the center of a dra- matic confrontation.[42] But after the scene at Rosings, when

Darcy's letter begins Elizabeth's movement toward self-recognition, the term "performance" quietly disappears from the novel. The first half of *Pride and Prejudice* has indeed been a dramatic performance, but in the second half a mixture of narrative, summary, and scene carries the plot toward its conclusion.

Yet this movement from the predominantly "scenic" construction of the first half of *Pride and Prejudice* into the less dramatic narrative of the second half does not lead to a drop in our interest, nor do we feel that the consistency of the novel's form has been violated. This is because the novel is unified by the indirect presence of Jane Austen's sensibility, and by the direct presence of Elizabeth Bennet as a commanding center of our interest. The shift from the scene at Rosings to Elizabeth's reception of Darcy's letter merely internalizes the drama; and the account of Elizabeth's changing reactions to Darcy's letter reminds us that Jane Austen has not renounced her right to record the inner life of a character with absolute authority. This is not to say that Elizabeth is a Jamesian "center of consciousness"; Jane Austen was too sure of her created world (and of its relation to the actual world) to efface her own personality from the novel, and from first sentence to last we are aware of the artist's command over her fictions. But her early experiments had shown the need for some technique that would counteract the novel's general tendency toward looseness of form by "focusing" action and psychological exposition, and in *The Watsons* she had explored the method of telling a story from the point-of-view of one character while reserving the right to qualify and expand that viewpoint through dramatic irony and direct comment. Such a method is really a compromise: it combines in a limited form the omniscience of traditional third-person narration with the immediacy of first-person narrative, giving the reader a sense of involvement and identification while simultaneously providing the perspective necessary for moral judgment. Of course, this method makes the exacting demand that the novel's central figure be perpetually intelligent and interesting, a demand which Jane Austen could only partially satisfy in *The Watsons*. But in revising *Pride and Prejudice* she created a heroine who could justify the form, and the result was a highly unified work in which the center of our interest is always at the center of the artistic composition.

IV

COUNTER-TRUTH

Mansfield Park

We know from Cassandra Austen's memorandum on the dates of her sister's novels that *Mansfield Park* was "begun somewhere about Feby 1811" and completed "soon after June 1813."[1] Thus Jane Austen's early work on *Mansfield Park* overlapped with the final revisions of *Pride and Prejudice*, and we may consider the two novels as counterstatements to each other. All the virtues of *Pride and Prejudice*—wit, irony, vitality, style—are transformed into the sins of *Mansfield Park*. Lionel Trilling has summed up the antagonism between the two works:

> . . . *Pride and Prejudice* makes comedy reverse itself and yield the implication of a divine enlargement. The novel celebrates the traits of spiritedness, vivacity, celerity, and lightness, and associates them with happiness and virtue. Its social doctrine is a generous one, asserting the right of at least the *good* individual to define himself according to his own essence. It is animated by an impulse to forgiveness. . . .
>
> Almost the opposite can be said of *Mansfield Park*. Its im-

pulse is not to forgive but to condemn. Its praise is not for social freedom but for social stasis. It takes full notice of spiritedness, vivacity, celerity, and lightness, but only to reject them as having nothing to do with virtue and happiness, as being, indeed, deterrents to the good life.[2]

Every critic who tries to chart the course of Jane Austen's artistic development must confront these contradictions, and it is not surprising that most are content to dismiss *Mansfield Park* as either "uncharacteristic" or "dishonest." The usual argument against *Mansfield Park* claims that novel is a deliberate rejection of the artist's true nature (as figured forth in *Pride and Prejudice*), a retreat from her characteristic irony and a betrayal of her generous and joyous nature which can only have been prompted by social pressures. The novel is viewed as a triumph of conventional morality over the perceptive artist.[3]

There is some justice in these criticisms. *Mansfield Park* is a strategic retreat from the exposed position of *Pride and Prejudice*, a retreat which is not—in terms of narrative structure—wholly successful. But Lionel Trilling, in the best essay yet written on the novel, has claimed that many of our objections to the novel are extra-literary, part of a failure to grant Jane Austen the artist's basic right of developing her chosen theme. Indeed, one cannot help feeling that most critics have placed *Mansfield Park* in a special category because the task of placing it in vital relation to the other novels would involve a challenge to their accepted judgments of those novels. But with Jane Austen, as with any great writer, each work must be seen through its companions, and in relation to the artist's entire career. If *Pride and Prejudice* and *Emma* emphasize the failures of *Mansfield Park*, so does *Mansfield Park* illuminate *their* limitations. One must remember that Jane Austen recognized other virtues than literary ones, and that irony and moral "style" were not her only values. In a sense, *Mansfield Park* is a consummate demonstration of the distinctions between literature and life.

One explanation for the radical differences between *Pride and Prejudice* and *Mansfield Park* is suggested by the histories of the two works. Although *Pride and Prejudice* was extensively reworked shortly before publication, the novel's essential dynamism—its gaiety and vitality—must have been inherited from the youthful *First Impressions*. Certainly the spirit of the *Juvenilia* and *Northanger Abbey* is carried forward, with greater subtlety and sophistication. But in *Mansfield Park* we are confronted with a product of Jane Austen's maturity. Parts of the novel may have been based on sketches or notes from the 1790's,[4] and the *donnée* of the "acting" motif lay in Jane Austen's early experience, but the attitudes and tone of *Mansfield Park* reflect the problems of her middle life. During the years between *First Impressions* and *Pride and Prejudice* she had grown from youth to middle-age, from the expectation of marriage into confirmed spinsterhood. Her secure home at Steventon had given way to the uncertainties of lodgings in Bath and Southampton, and only recently— with the move to Chawton—had the family been re-established in congenial surroundings. Her father had died, there had been many changes in the close-knit family, and the assumptions of rural English society were no longer quite the same. There is also some evidence that Jane Austen had overcome her early objections to Evangelical religion and was even attracted by it.[5] In short, the mature artist who completed *Pride and Prejudice* in 1811–12 was far removed from the young girl who began *First Impressions*; and although she could still appreciate and extend the sparkling qualities of that work, when she undertook her first new creation since the unfinished *Watsons* the result was "a complete change of subject," [6] a novel which embodied a new range of experience and was deliberately conceived as a counterbalance to *Pride and Prejudice*. On 4 February 1813 she wrote to Cassandra of *Pride and Prejudice*:

> The work is rather too light, and bright, and sparkling; it wants shade; it wants to be stretched out here and there with a long chapter of sense, if it could be had; if not, of solemn specious nonsense, about something unconnected with the story; an essay on writing, a critique on Walter Scott, or the history of Buonaparté, or anything that would form a contrast, and bring the reader with increased delight to the playfulness and epigrammatism of the general style.

Beneath this playful and apparently self-satisfied critique of *Pride and Prejudice* we sense a deep dissatisfaction with its want of "shade," a dissatisfaction which found full—one might almost say exaggerated—expression in *Mansfield Park*.

This growing reaction against the confident irony of her early fiction, against that which is "light, and bright, and sparkling" at the expense of decorum and sense, is reflected in some of the erasures in the *Juvenilia*. For example, the following parody in *Volume the First* was completely erased sometime after its composition:

A Fragment
written to inculcate the practise of Virtue

We all know that many are unfortunate in their progress through the world, but we do not know all that are so. To seek them out to study their wants, & to leave them unsupplied is the duty, and ought to be the Business of Man. But few have time, fewer still have inclination, and no one has either the one or the other for such employments. Who amidst those that perspire away their Evenings in crouded assemblies can have

> leisure to bestow a thought on such as sweat under the fatigue
> of their daily Labour. (71)

This ironic commentary on didactic fiction was probably excised because it came too close to a mockery of those conventional moral attitudes which Jane Austen grew to appreciate.
The reaction against this passage shows a developing awareness of the danger inherent in ironic methods, the possibility
that mockery of pretensions will become a mockery of the solid
virtues those pretensions distort. In *Pride and Prejudice* irony
can be turned into an agency for self-knowledge, but in *Mansfield Park* we see that it can also be a buttress for cynicism.
"Wisdom is better than Wit" [7] could well be the motto of
Mansfield Park.

If *Mansfield Park* were not flanked so closely by *Pride and
Prejudice* and *Emma* it might be possible to view the novel
simply as a product of "an unusual state of the author's
mind." [8] But the fact that Jane Austen could work almost
simultaneously on *Pride and Prejudice,* and turn so quickly to
Emma, suggests that *Mansfield Park* does not represent an
unusual state of the author's mind so much as one basic tendency of her mind given unusually free play. To say this is not
merely to quibble with words. Throughout Jane Austen's
works, from the *Juvenilia* to *Sanditon,* we can discover a tension between two fundamental attitudes which may be called,
for want of better terms, neoclassicism and romanticism. One
attitude embodies the claims of society, the other the claims
of the individual; one stresses reason, the other imagination.
The puzzle of *Mansfield Park* is not that it emphasizes one
side of this dialectic, as a corrective to *Pride and Prejudice,*
but that the expression is so uncompromising. For once in Jane
Austen's art the familiar tensions and qualifications are resolved into bald didacticism. Even the somber tone of her
middle years seems inadequate justification for this arbitrary

resolution, and one can understand the dissatisfaction which has driven many critics to speculate on specific biographical sources for the narrow and direct vision of *Mansfield Park*. So much of the indignation in *Mansfield Park* appears disproportionate to its subject—I am thinking especially of the "acting" controversy—that it is natural to seek the source of this indignation outside the novel. Such expeditions are usually futile, but in the case of *Mansfield Park* one possible "source" casts so much light on the novel's major themes that it deserves our consideration, regardless of whether Jane Austen held it consciously in mind.

Among Jane Austen's friends and acquaintances the most promising prototype for Mary Crawford is her cousin Eliza de Feuillide (formerly Eliza Hancock), whose husband, the Comte de Feuillide, was guillotined in 1794.[9] She later married Henry Austen, and Jane was intimately familiar with her character and every detail of her spectacular career. Eliza participated in the family theatricals at Steventon when Jane was an eager twelve-year-old spectator, and her influence seems to have been decisive in persuading Henry Austen to give up his early thoughts of the Church (after the death of Eliza in 1813 he did take orders). In Eliza's relationship with another cousin, Philadelphia Walter, we find a close approximation of the relationship between Mary Crawford and Fanny Price, and Eliza's personality reminds us of Mary's high-spirited, flirtatious nature. There can, of course, be no question of a direct portrayal; Eliza Austen was still alive when *Mansfield Park* was written, and Jane Austen would never have pained her brother with a recognizable portrait. As R. W. Chapman has reminded us, no one in the family thought Mary Crawford a portrayal of Eliza;[10] but any reader of Eliza's letters to Philadelphia Walter will recognize the qualities that Jane Austen emphasized in her fiction, and will realize that the basic problems of *Mansfield Park* were neither improbable nor foreign to Jane Austen's experience. Whether Jane Austen did or did not have her cousin in mind is much less important than the clear evidence that the dilemma of *Mansfield Park* was of vital contemporary interest, part of a clash between traditional notions of decorum and a growing emphasis on freedom of personal expression.

In 1786 Eliza de Feuillide came to England to give birth to her first child. She had been six years in France, five of them as the wife of a French nobleman, and to her cousins she appeared as the epitome of fashion and elegance. In September 1787 she and her mother took her cousin Philadelphia Walter to Tunbridge Wells; here is Philadelphia's account of the visit.

> I had spent ten days with them at the Wells. They came here and staid one night when I returned with them and lived a gayer life than I ever before experienced, enjoyments for every hour; for a few first days I was miserable, and would have given anything to have got away to any retired corner, but their very great kindness, affection and attention to me soon reconciled me to the dissipated life they led and put me in mind that every woman is at heart a rake. . . . In the evening to the play which my cousin bespoke and was *Which is the Man?* and *Bon Ton* . . . You will expect my opinion of my friends. . . . The Countess has many amiable qualities, such as the highest duty, love and respect for her mother: for whom there is not any sacrifice she would not make, & certainly contributes entirely to her happiness: for her husband she professes a large share of respect, esteem and the highest opinion of his merits, but confesses that Love is not of the number on her side, tho' still very violent on his: her principles are strictly just, making it a rule never to bespeak anything that she is not quite sure of being able to pay for directly, never contracting debts of any kind. Her dissipated life she was brought up to—therefore it cannot be wondered at . . . They go at Xmas to Steventon & mean to

act a play *Which is the Man?* and *Bon Ton.* My uncle's barn is fitting up quite like a theatre, & all the young folks are to take their part. The Countess is Lady Bob Lardoon [presumably an error for Lady Bell Bloomer] in the former and Miss Tittup in the latter. They wish me much of the party & offer to carry me, but I do not think of it. I should like to be a spectator, but am sure I should not have courage to act a part, nor do I wish to attain it . . .[11]

Phila's resolution not to join the theatricals could not be broken. In November Eliza wrote to her begging that she reconsider:

> You cannot possibly resist so many temptations, especially when I tell you your old friend James is returned from France & is to be of the acting party . . .[12]

And this was followed by another plea:

> I will only allow myself to take notice of the strong reluctance you express to what you call *appearing in Publick.* I assure you our performance is to be by no means a publick one, since only a select party of friends will be present. . . . You wish to know the exact time which we should be *satisfied with* & therefore I proceed to acquaint you that a fortnight from New Year's Day *would do,* provided however you could bring yourself to act . . .[13]

In this exchange Phila's moral scruples and spectatorial attitude are strongly suggestive of Fanny Price, and the arguments against amateur theatricals are those of *Mansfield Park*. Phila's reluctance to "act a part" is identical with Fanny's protestation, "No, indeed, I cannot act" (145), and possesses the same moral overtones. As we shall see, the themes of "acting" and imitation lie at the center of *Mansfield Park,* and justify the

elaborate narrative device of the play. Knowing that amateur
theatricals were a favorite amusement at Steventon, many
readers have been baffled by the objections to "acting" in
Mansfield Park. It is well to remember that Jane Austen was
familiar with Philadelphia's objections to these performances,
and that in the light of subsequent events she may have come
to share them. There is no doubt that she, like Edmund Bertram, always appreciated "good hardened real acting" by pro-
fessionals (124), but this does not mean that her youthful
delight in amateur theatricals was long enduring. Perhaps
the subsequent correspondence between Eliza and Philadelphia will illuminate this shift in attitude.

The fact that the plays to be presented at Steventon in
Christmas 1787 were the same two "bespoke" by Eliza at
Tunbridge Wells suggests that she made the choice, and the
parts she was to play confirm her love of flirtation. The young
Jane Austen must have been clearly aware of the influence
her beautiful cousin exercised over Henry and James Austen,
and there was a tradition in later generations of the Austen
family that Eliza's marriage to Henry in 1797 was the outcome
of renewed theatrical parties at Steventon.[14] It seems fairly
certain that Eliza wished Henry to abandon his plans for the
Church, since in May 1797 she wrote to Philadelphia:

> I suppose you know that our cousin Henry is now Captain,
> Paymaster, & Adjutant. He is a very lucky young man & bids
> fair to possess a considerable share of riches & honours. I be-
> lieve he has now given up all thoughts of the Church, & he is
> right for he certainly is not so fit for a parson as a soldier. . . .[15]

The implication is that Henry's decision to give up "all
thoughts of the Church" was not entirely his own: seven
months later he and Eliza were married.

From Eliza's letters to Philadelphia we gain a clear picture

of a complex and fascinating personality not unlike Mary
Crawford's. Eliza's mind was lively, with a turn for irony, and
she was endowed with remarkable self-knowledge. In contrast
to her Philadelphia appears rather drab and prim, hedged
about by strict notions of propriety and decorum. It is easy to
believe that the youthful Jane Austen found Eliza delightful
and Philadelphia rather dull; on first meeting her cousins in
1788 Philadelphia was attracted to Cassandra but considered
Jane "whimsical & affected." [16] Yet it seems likely that as Jane
grew older her opinion of Eliza changed, and while she never
lost her fondness for her sister-in-law she came to understand
Philadelphia's position as well. In "The Three Sisters" of
Volume the First the ill-natured and mean Mary Stanhope
demands of her future husband:

> "You must build a room on purpose & a Theatre to act Plays in.
> The first Play we have shall be *Which is the Man*, and I will
> do Lady Bell Bloomer." (65)

Although Eliza may never have played the real-life role of
Lady Bell, the seductive widow in Mrs. Cowley's play, there
is a strong possibility that Jane Austen resented her influence
over Henry, and that the problem of "ordination" in *Mansfield Park*—which is connected, as Lionel Trilling has demonstrated, with the question of "acting a part" in life [17]—had its
origin in Eliza's opposition to Henry's "thoughts of the
Church." But whether one accepts these biographical arguments or not, the correspondence between Eliza and Philadelphia shows that the reaction of Edmund and Fanny to the
amateur production of *Lovers' Vows* is rooted in a distrust of
"acting" with which Jane Austen was familiar, and which has
little to do with the specific content of the play. Indeed, the
debate over amateur theatricals which dominates the first
volume of *Mansfield Park* is so complicated, and Jane Austen's

artistic use of the debate so cunning, that any interpretation
of the novel must begin from that point.

The play that Mr. Yates brings to Mansfield, Kotzebue's
Lovers' Vows (*Das Kind der Liebe*), was published in Ger-
many in 1791. Between 1798 and 1800 at least four adaptations of it appeared in English, but only one of these, that of
Mrs. Inchbald, "seems to have been performed, and there is
no doubt of its being the *Lovers' Vows* of *Mansfield Park*, for
the quotation on page 358 agrees with Mrs. Inchbald's text,
and the number of Count Cassel's speeches is just two-and-
forty." [18] Mrs. Inchbald's "translation" was actually a free
adaptation trimmed to fit current taste, as she openly admits in
her Preface; and her success in meeting this taste is evidenced
by the play's great popularity. It was an immediate success,
and was still being performed as late as the 1830's.[19] Mrs.
Inchbald's version ran through twelve editions in less than two
years, and was frequently reprinted after 1800. It seems almost
certain that Jane Austen witnessed a professional production
of *Lovers' Vows,* since it was performed six times at the Theatre Royal in Bath during the years (1801–05) when she
lived there.[20]

The abortive play-acting in *Mansfield Park,* which provides
a focus for the first third of the novel and conditions our initial
responses to all the characters, is a consummate example of
Jane Austen's constructional skill. In writing *Mansfield Park*
she was confronted with a more intricate situation, and a
wider range of characters, than in any of her previous works.
The first volume immediately introduces us to a full cast of
characters, none of whom (least of all the intended heroine)
are fully developed in isolation. Jane Austen needed some device that would precipitate an emotional crisis and thus bring
into focus the latent distinctions among the characters: in
effect, an "artificial" polarization of the novel's moral attitudes.
The amateur theatricals provided this device. The theatrical

project quickens the novel's personal relationships, establishes Fanny's position as spectator, and prefigures the later course of action. Jane Austen's resort to this almost mechanical device confirms our impression of her god-like role in the novel, her failure to make direct contact with the characters, while at the same time it forces us to a new appreciation of her dramatic talent.

Although it is not necessary to know the plot of Lovers' Vows in order to understand the first crisis in the novel, a familiarity with the play sharpens our insight into Edmund's moral dilemma and helps us to grasp the novel's structural unity. In Lovers' Vows the soldier-hero, Frederick, returns home after an absence of five years to find his mother, Agatha Friburg, destitute outside an inn. Frederick needs a birth certificate for military purposes, and his mother is forced to confess that he is the natural son of Baron Wildenhaim. Since Frederick has no money with which to help his mother, he is reduced to begging. In desperation he attempts to obtain money by force, but is taken prisoner and confined to a castle, where he learns that his intended victim—now his captor—is Baron Wildenhaim. Aided by a young clergyman named Anhalt, who is tutor to the Baron's daughter Amelia, Frederick persuades the Baron to acknowledge his son and marry Agatha (the Baron's former wife, Amelia's mother, has recently died). This is the main plot of Lovers' Vows; the subsidiary plot concerns Amelia, who is finally united with her lover Anhalt, after overcoming her father's desire that she marry the foolish Count Cassel.

It would be too much to say—as one critic has—that there is a point-by-point correspondence between the action of Mansfield Park and the plot of Lovers' Vows,[21] but it is true that the "dramatic roles" adopted by the young people at Mansfield foreshadow the parts they are to play in the remainder of the novel. A Dramatis Personae for the ill-fated play will make this clear:

Lovers' Vows	Mansfield Park
Baron Wildenhaim	Mr. Yates
Agatha	Maria Bertram
Frederick	Henry Crawford
Count Cassel	Mr. Rushworth
Amelia	Mary Crawford
Anhalt	Edmund Bertram
Butler Landlord Cottager	Tom Bertram
Cottager's Wife	Mrs. Grant

In several cases, the casting is a clue to character. Mr. Rushworth's ineffectual and foolish nature is paralleled in the foppery of Count Cassel, while Tom Bertram's obliging but rather weak personality is reflected in his triple role. The "forward" manner of Amelia, which Mrs. Inchbald deplored in her Preface and attempted to rectify in her translation, reinforces our impression of Mary Crawford. But other roles go beyond the immediate service of characterization, and have prophetic overtones. Mr. Yates's folly (the elopement) and ultimate repentance are prefigured in the career of the Baron, with his initial irresponsibility and last-act change of heart; and Maria's seduction is foreshadowed in the role of Agatha. Perhaps the most subtle presentiment lies in Edmund's vacillation between the attractions of Mary Crawford and his reluctance to act the part of a clergyman, Anhalt. One must remember that Mary views *ordination* as merely the assumption of a social role, while to Edmund it signifies the beginning of a life-long vocation.

On a more general level, *Lovers' Vows* poses the basic moral problems of the novel. In Kotzebue's play the sympathetic imagination runs riot, resulting in a drama of sentimental pathos. Moral judgment and "poetic justice" have been washed away in a flood of uncontrolled feeling. No general standard of conduct rules the work, good intentions are equal to good actions, and—to use Coleridge's words—the play appeals "by a pathos not a whit more respectable than the maudlin tears of drunkenness." [22] With its emphasis on feeling and disregard for traditional restraints, with its contempt for social form, *Lovers' Vows* stands as an emblem of those forces which threaten the neoclassical security of Mansfield Park. Jane Austen has returned to the dialectic of *Sense and Sensibility,* but with a narrow intensity which is in startling contrast to the liberal tone of *Pride and Prejudice.*

But if, in her rejection of *Lovers' Vows,* with its Rousseauistic values and shoddy emotionalism, Jane Austen allied herself with the narrow moralists of her age, it was not because she shared all their premises. Contemporary objections to the play centered on its lack of "poetic justice," as in the criticism of William Cobbett's *Porcupine:*

> The fall of Agatha . . . is effected too easily; and her restoration to happiness, notwithstanding her repentance, forms too much of an apology for error. Such things may be admitted in real life; but, on the stage, a seduced female should never be suffered to appear but as an object of terror.[23]

In *Mansfield Park,* however, the interest does not lie in the impact of the play upon its audience, but in the effect of "acting" upon amateur players. In Edmund's eyes, the danger stems not from the theater as such, but from the impact of a "performance" upon players "who have all the disadvantages of education and decorum to struggle through" (124). Again and again the word "decorum" is invoked, and Lionel Trilling is surely right when he locates the decisive argument against "acting" not in the language or actions of the play, but in "a traditional, almost primitive, feeling about dramatic impersonation," a rejection of the romantic notion that "personality" is the sum of the roles we play.[24] We are reminded of Philadelphia Walter's reluctance to "act a part," and can see that Jane Austen's mature attitude toward amateur theatricals, instead of being a mysterious departure from her early enthusiasm, may have grown directly out of her experiences at Steventon.

The plays upon the word "acting" in *Mansfield Park* are so persistent, and so much a part of the novel's major themes, that they deserve special consideration. As the novel progresses the ability "to act a part" becomes a touchstone to insincerity, so that Fanny's early, horrified protest, "No, indeed, I cannot act" (145), finally becomes a moral accolade, while Crawford's reputation as "considerably the best actor of all" (165) is seen in retrospect as a warning of his basic insincerity. Maria acts "well—too well" (165). When Henry Crawford reads in a "truly dramatic" fashion from Shakespeare, recalling to Fanny's mind "all his acting," the word is already rich in moral overtones; for a moment Fanny is captivated by Crawford's fluency, and can even look back with pleasure at his performance in *Lovers' Vows*.

> . . . in Mr. Crawford's reading there was a variety of excellence beyond what she had ever met with. The King, the Queen, Buckingham, Wolsey, Cromwell, all were given in turn; for with the happiest knack, the happiest power of jumping and guessing, he could always light, at will, on the best scene, or the best speeches of each; and whether it were dignity or pride, or tenderness or remorse, or whatever were to be expressed, he could do it with equal beauty.—It was truly dramatic.—His acting had first taught Fanny what pleasure a play might give, and his reading brought all his acting before her again; nay, perhaps with greater enjoyment, for it came unex-

pectedly, and with no such drawback as she had been used to suffer in seeing him on the stage with Miss Bertram. (337)

Fanny does not recollect herself until the conversation turns to ordination, with Crawford insisting that the liturgy requires "good reading" and that sermons must be judged as "performances."

> "A sermon, well delivered, is more uncommon even than prayers well read. A sermon, good in itself, is no rare thing. It is more difficult to speak well than to compose well; that is, the rules and tricks of composition are oftener an object of study. A thoroughly good sermon, thoroughly well delivered, is a capital gratification. I can never hear such a one without the greatest admiration and respect, and more than half a mind to take orders and preach. There is something in the eloquence of the pulpit, when it is really eloquence, which is entitled to the highest praise and honour. The preacher who can touch and affect such an heterogeneous mass of hearers, on subjects limited, and long worn thread-bare in all common hands; who can say any thing new or striking, any thing that rouses the attention, without offending the taste, or wearing out the feelings of his hearers, is a man whom one could not (in his public capacity) honour enough. I should like to be such a man." (341)

Crawford can imagine himself in the role of preacher, but his disregard of the reality behind that role informs Fanny of his true nature. Similarly, when Mary Crawford recalls with pleasure "that acting week" when she first made sympathetic contact with Edmund (358), we are reminded that her interest has always been in the appearance of things.

The distinction between genuine emotion and the impersonation of feeling is never more clearly before us than in the contrasting reports of Tom's illness which Fanny receives while at Portsmouth. Her aunt's letters, dramatizing second-hand information, are all "a sort of playing at being frightened" (427); Lady Bertram's imagination can only produce the stock responses of sentimental drama. She cannot write with genuine emotion or concern until Tom is actually before her eyes, but then her letter, "which she had been previously preparing for Fanny, was finished in a different style, in the language of real feeling and alarm."

> "He is just come, my dear Fanny, and is taken up stairs; and I am so shocked to see him, that I do not know what to do. I am sure he has been very ill. Poor Tom, I am quite grieved for him, and very much frightened, and so is Sir Thomas; and how glad I should be, if you were here to comfort me." (427)

The imagination, presented in Jane Austen's other works as a possible source of enlightenment and love, seems bound in *Mansfield Park* to the service of hypocrisy.

In *Pride and Prejudice* the hero and heroine seek to achieve freedom by asserting their ideals within the stubborn forms of society. As in all great novels of manners, the limitations of society are acknowledged, but within these limitations Darcy and Elizabeth (like Mirabell and Millamant before them) create the illusion of freedom. *Pride and Prejudice* is Frost's constant symbol, "a figure of the will braving alien entanglements." Decorum is seen as necessary, but it must be decorum that allows room for individual freedom. Elizabeth and Darcy are both skilled actors, and like good actors they cause us to forget the restrictions which surround them. In contrast, *Mansfield Park* offers the paradox that freedom can only come through constant self-limitation. To borrow T. S. Eliot's phrase, life at Mansfield Park is the classic "escape from personality" rather than an expression of personality; and the failure of Sir Thomas lies not in his strictness but in his failure to enforce his own stern ideals, to purge Mansfield of the easy freedom promoted by Mrs. Norris. Like the Gothic novel,

Lovers' Vows offers to the imagination starved by restraint an escape into a world of violence and passion, yet such an escape is too easily translated into terms of real life, as the play is translated into the action of the novel. In a sense Jane Austen has returned to the problem of *Northanger Abbey,* but with a different point-of-view. Mansfield Park offers refuge from the demands of the imagination. The play is brought from the outside world, like a moral infection, and must be taken as a symbol of the dangers that lurk within the imagination. Elizabeth and Darcy know that they are not free, but they manage to create the illusion of freedom. *Mansfield Park* exposes the dangers of that illusion.

Jane Austen took for the heroine of *Mansfield Park* a girl who is essentially passive and uninteresting, and in so doing she deliberately rejected the principle of growth and change which animates most English fiction. Fanny is the antithesis of the conventional heroine, the reverse of Pamela, a young woman who declines the role of Cinderella.[25] Given the bourgeois origins of the English novel, and the large female reading public, it is not surprising that the Cinderella story should underlie so many works. Jane Austen's novels are no exception to this, and in Elizabeth's triumph over Lady Catherine, and marriage to Darcy, the universal fantasy is satisfied. But *Mansfield Park* destroys this fantasy, and deprives the reader of the fundamental pleasure of wish-fulfillment. The novel is furnished with all the characters of the Cinderella legend, but in the end the charming lover is rejected. This denial of the fairy tale could be related to the frustrations of a spinster approaching forty, but on another—and more interesting—level the reversal of the fairy tale may be seen as part of a general attack on the dangers of "fiction." At its deepest reaches *Mansfield Park* questions the motives and consolations of art itself.

Perhaps this last statement holds the key to the novel's fail-

ures of style and structure. In many ways *Mansfield Park* is a
more skilled production than the earlier novels, and if we
knew nothing of its origins we would still have to date it, on
technical evidence alone, after *Pride and Prejudice*. The construction of the first volume is a tour de force. Having set herself the task of presenting a passive heroine whose personality
(unlike that of Mary Crawford) is hardly compelling, Jane
Austen was cut off from the brilliant manipulation of dialogue
which holds our attention in the first volume of *Pride and
Prejudice;* but through the device of the play she manages to
keep Fanny at the center of the action while setting in motion
what is essentially a drama of ideas. And after the first volume
she succeeds in maintaining this focus by allowing us to see
the events through Fanny's eyes, with her reactions as a kind
of chorus. Nor is the novel lacking in perceptive observation;
the shabby home at Portsmouth is rendered with a direct
realism that makes us feel all its depressing qualities. But in
spite of these technical achievements *Mansfield Park* lacks a
sustained vitality. The problem is one of tone, most of all, and
is related to the novel's general themes. In a work which questions the values of wit and imagination, which seems to say
that virtue must involve dullness, the redeeming force can
only be the author's presiding personality, and this Jane Austen
refuses—or is unable—to assert. The form of *Mansfield Park*
expresses all too clearly its author's conviction that the values
of art are not the ultimate ones.

But to call the tone of *Mansfield Park* a "betrayal" is to set
an arbitrary standard, to ignore the dialectic of the earlier
works and the position of *Mansfield Park* in Jane Austen's development as an artist. We have seen that in her *Juvenilia*
Jane Austen experimented with various means for dramatizing
the conflicting claims of imagination and reason, of the individual will and social forms, and that these experiments were
part of a process of self-discovery. In *Northanger Abbey* she

explored the uses of the imagination, which can either serve or distort reality. In *Sense and Sensibility* the conflict was schematized and defined, but not resolved. With *Pride and Prejudice,* however, the recurrent debate was brought to an attractive resolution; the novel's formal unity became a symbol of the unified personality, and its irony established a balance where before there had been tension and conflict. But, for a number of complex reasons involving both her life and her art, Jane Austen could not rest on the easy assurance of *Pride and Prejudice,* which shuns tragic implications and satisfies our most cherished fantasies. In short, *Pride and Prejudice* did not satisfy her mature sense of reality, and in *Mansfield Park* she gave direct expression to all that was left out of *Pride and Prejudice.* Evidently the writing of *Mansfield Park* was a necessary catharsis for Jane Austen, since in her next novel, *Emma,* she was able to encompass and extend the themes of all her previous works.

V

THE LIMITS OF FREEDOM

Emma

In her work on *Emma* Jane Austen regained the vigor and charm of *Pride and Prejudice* without sacrificing the moral imperatives of *Mansfield Park*. The antagonism between art and morality which weakens so much of *Mansfield Park*—an antagonism reminiscent of eighteenth-century attacks on the irresponsibility of fiction—has been replaced in *Emma* by a renewed faith in the powers of art, a serene belief that the novel can both recreate and criticize the illusions of life. One might say that in *Emma* Jane Austen achieved the means for expressing that synthesis of opposing values which had long been her goal. Such a synthesis was sure to affront the average reader's expectations, and Jane Austen was acutely aware of this danger: "I am very strongly haunted with the idea that to those readers who have preferred 'Pride and Prejudice' it will appear inferior in wit, and to those who have preferred 'Mansfield Park' very inferior in good sense." [1] Here wit must have the meaning of lightness or sharp repartee, and we are reminded of Jane Austen's half-serious complaint that *Pride and Prejudice* "is rather too light, and bright, and sparkling; it wants shade; it wants to be stretched out here and there with a long chapter of sense . . . anything that would form a contrast, and bring the reader with increased delight to the playfulness and epigrammatism of the general style." [2] In *Pride and Prejudice* she had created a heroine whose personality threatened to eclipse the novel's moral judgments, while in *Mansfield Park* she had committed the opposite error. It was only with *Emma* that she fully developed those narrative techniques that enabled her to exercise continuous—and often adverse—moral judgments on her heroine without detracting from the force of the heroine's personality. And yet, in spite of this triumphant mating of form and purpose, she knew that the resulting complexity would be a shock to the audience whose expectations were drawn from contemporary fiction, or even from her own earlier works: "I am going to take a heroine whom no one but myself will much like." [3]

The basic movement of *Emma* is from delusion to self-recognition, from illusion to reality.[4] The three major stages in the drama, corresponding roughly to the novel's three volumes, concern Emma's "blindness" to the real natures of Mr. Elton, Frank Churchill, and finally Mr. Knightley; but all these errors of judgment are functions of her fundamental lack of self-understanding. Emma is an "imaginist" (335) who "sets up . . . for Understanding" (427), only to be subjected to a series of shocks which gradually brings her to grips with reality. The pattern of *Emma* resembles in many ways the pattern of the first half of *Pride and Prejudice,* which culminates in Darcy's letter and Elizabeth's recognition that "Till this moment, I never knew myself" (208); but it is a sign of the differences between the two novels that the problem of self-recognition occupies the entire course of *Emma,* while after Elizabeth's moment of self-understanding the interest in *Pride and Prejudice* shifts from personal problems of judgment to

CONCLUSION

the social problems of communication and reconciliation. In
Pride and Prejudice the fault of vision, once corrected, is taken
as fully overcome, whereas in *Emma* life is presented as a constant process of emotional miscalculations and rational corrections. Even after her final disillusionment with Harriet we
find Emma unconsciously planning a match between Mrs.
Weston's daughter and "either of Isabella's sons" (461), and
we must trust in Knightley's continuing power to control
Emma's penchant for manipulating life.

In *Emma* the conflicts between Fancy and Understanding,
Feeling and Reason, which dominate the earlier fiction, are
still in command, but they are internalized within one character. The terms for Emma's vacillating emotions are furnished
by Mr. Knightley:

> "Emma has been meaning to read more ever since she was
> twelve years old. I have seen a great many lists of her drawing
> up at various times of books that she meant to read regularly
> through—and very good lists they were—very well chosen, and
> very neatly arranged—sometimes alphabetically, and sometimes
> by some other rule. The list she drew up when only fourteen—I
> remember thinking it did her judgment so much credit, that I
> preserved it some time; and I dare say she may have made out
> a very good list now. But I have done with expecting any course
> of steady reading from Emma. She will never submit to any
> thing requiring industry and patience, and a subjection of the
> fancy to the understanding." (37)

Knightley's vocabulary of judgment, familiar to us from the
earlier novels, is also Emma's, and her self-deceptions are cast
in its terms. What distinguishes *Emma* from a work such as
Sense and Sensibility is the fact that the philosophic debate
has been completely realized in human action. Mr. Knightley,
who succeeds in the fatherly role where Sir Thomas Bertram
failed, is able to act as a moral chorus without diminishing our

sense of his reality. Instead of standing as Emma's opponent or censor, he represents the native good sense which is obscured by her abuse of reason. Through Knightley the world of *Mansfield Park* enters *Emma*, but without any sense of oppression or self-denial, for he is liberating something within Emma herself.

C. S. Lewis has remarked that "the greatest of all divisions in the history of the West" is that which divides the age of Jane Austen from our own age.[5] In some ways this is true, especially if we think of Jane Austen's novels as a summing-up of the classic eighteenth-century debates, a repository of notions concerning moral propriety and social decorum which were obsolescent in her own day. But to read the novels in this fashion is to ignore the many ways in which they seem closer to our own time than to the age of Fielding and Richardson, or even Fanny Burney; and this "modernity" does not lie entirely in the realm of narrative method. Within Emma Woodhouse we discern the forces that will produce Emma Bovary, and all those other nineteenth-century heroines whose illusions can only end in tragedy. Jane Austen carefully limits the tragic potential of her heroine, imposing "classic" restraint upon the "romantic" imagination, but she does not obscure the dangers in Emma's illusions. Although Emma may resemble Catherine Morland in her romanticization of Harriet's origins, and of the encounter with the gypsies, her fictions are considerably less innocent than those of the passive Catherine. Not only is she determined to act upon them, but she is eager to impose them upon others. In the tradition of the Quixotic heroine, Emma Woodhouse stands halfway between Cervantes and Flaubert, sharing the characteristics of both Don Quixote and Emma Bovary.[6] Within the restricted world of Highbury she aspires to a god-like role.

In *"Sensus Communis:* An Essay on the Freedom of Wit and Humour" (I. iv) Shaftesbury says that the "natural free

Spirits of ingenious Men, if imprison'd and controul'd, will find out other ways of Motion to relieve themselves in their *Constraint.* . . ." One release, that of Jane Austen herself, is through wit and humour, the play of irony; another, and this is Emma's release, is through the play of fancy, illusion-mongering, and irresponsible match-making. The problem Jane Austen confronts is this: how can one accept the re-straints symbolized by Mansfield Park without destroying the creative imagination and free inquiry of a personality such as Emma's? One spurious release, as we have seen, comes through vicarious enjoyment of Gothic violence and the cult of sensibility; another, and this is Emma's, lies in the attempt to transcend social and personal limitations through the power of the individual will. In *Mansfield Park* the conflict between classic decorum and the demands of the individual personality is solved through a suppression of personality. But in *Emma,* where Jane Austen gives fullest value to both imagination and reason, we are left with the paradox that freedom can only be achieved *through* self-restraint and self-knowledge. The nega-tive morality of *Mansfield Park* has been transformed by an active interest in self-fulfillment which reminds us of *Pride and Prejudice.*

If we examine the stages of Emma's movement toward self-recognition we find that she is deceived as to the outside world (Don Quixote) and deceived as to her own emotions (Emma Bovary), and that the two kinds of deception are related. In her wrong assessment of Mr. Elton's intentions, Emma's ability to judge external reality is subtly distorted by her desire that he shall love Harriet Smith. She is "too eager and busy in her own previous conceptions and views to hear him impartially, or see him with clear vision" (110). Long before Elton's pro-posal destroys Emma's illusion the reader has been led through a series of ironic revelations to an exact assessment of her de-

pendence on "previous conceptions," and her unwillingness
to acknowledge her own limitations. Her "improved" drawing
of Harriet suggests her desire to shape Harriet's destiny; and
Knightley's criticism of the distortion in the picture touches
Emma's good sense, although she is too proud to acknowledge
its truth in public.

> "You have made her too tall, Emma," said Mr. Knightley.
> Emma knew that she had, but would not own it, and Mr.
> Elton warmly added,
> "Oh, no! certainly not too tall; not in the least too tall. . . .
> Proportions, fore-shortening.—Oh, no! it gives one exactly the
> idea of such a height as Miss Smith's. Exactly so indeed!" (48)

The episode of the drawing places the characters in relation
to each other, and establishes Knightley's role as critical
guardian of Emma's ambitious imagination. Similarly, the
affair of the charade (71-3) helps to define Emma's willful
misreading of reality; her "previous conceptions" blind her
to the obvious meaning of Elton's verse. Jane Austen allows
Emma to reveal herself, and the reader is gradually led to an
easy acceptance of the author's point-of-view.

In the next stage of her development, after the humiliating
recognition of Mr. Elton's true intentions, Emma is still confident of her own insight. Unlike Mr. Knightley, she never
allows her judgment to be softened by a memory of Cowper's
line, "Myself creating what I saw." Her total misunderstanding of Jane Fairfax, based partly on envy and partly on a vain
delight in Frank Churchill's attentions, is neatly dramatized
in the scene where she produces an ingenious explanation for
the gift of the pianoforte. Unaware of Frank Churchill's secret
engagement to Miss Fairfax, Emma cannot suspect that the
piano was a gift from him; but in her mischievous desire to
expose Jane Fairfax she concocts a more fanciful explanation.

"The arrival of this pianoforté is decisive with me [said Emma]. I wanted to know a little more, and this tells me quite enough. Depend upon it, we shall soon hear that it is a present from Mr. and Mrs. Dixon."

"And if the Dixons should absolutely deny all knowledge of it [replied Frank Churchill] we must conclude it to come from the Campbells."

"No, I am sure it is not from the Campbells. Miss Fairfax knows it is not from the Campbells, or they would have been guessed at first. She would not have been puzzled, had she dared fix on them. I may not have convinced you perhaps, but I am perfectly convinced myself that Mr. Dixon is a principal in the business."

"Indeed you injure me if you suppose me unconvinced. Your reasonings carry my judgment along with them entirely. At first, while I supposed you satisfied that Col. Campbell was the giver, I saw it only as paternal kindness, and thought it the most natural thing in the world. But when you mentioned Mrs. Dixon, I felt how much more probable that it should be the tribute of warm female friendship. And now I can see it in no other light than as an offering of love." (218–19)

The irony in this exchange is entirely at Emma's expense, and her memory of it is part of her punishment. Ultimately she must realize that she has viewed life as a game in which she can display her imagination and powers of perception; it is no accident that Jane Austen uses Emma's fondness for conundrums, charades, and word-games to reveal her errors of imagination. This particular motif culminates early in the third volume, in a scene at Hartfield (343–51). Mr. Knightley has already begun to suspect an attachment between Frank Churchill and Jane Fairfax, although still distrustful of his imagination; and Frank has nearly revealed his secret by a careless allusion to information supplied in a letter from Miss Fairfax. To cover his confusion and distract the company from his error, Frank Churchill proposes that they play the word-game. Emma is pleased at this opportunity to display her skill, and is blind to Jane's embarrassment when Frank presents her with an anagram for "blunder." Mr. Knightley, aware of the genuine emotions at stake in the game, is an indignant specta-tor as Frank Churchill plays upon Emma's preconceptions.

> He [Mr. Knightley] saw a short word prepared for Emma, and given to her with a look sly and demure. He saw that Emma had soon made it out, and found it highly entertaining, though it was something which she judged it proper to appear to censure; for she said, "Nonsense! for shame!" He heard Frank Churchill next say, with a glance towards Jane, "I will give it to her—shall I?"—and as clearly heard Emma opposing it with eager laughing warmth. "No, no, you must not; you shall not, indeed."
>
> It was done however. This gallant young man, who seemed to love without feeling, and to recommend himself without complaisance, directly handed over the word to Miss Fairfax, and with a particular degree of sedate civility entreated her to study it. Mr. Knightley's excessive curiosity to know what this word might be, made him seize every possible moment for dart-ing his eye towards it, and it was not long before he saw it to be *Dixon.* Jane Fairfax's perception seemed to accompany his; her comprehension was certainly more equal to the covert mean-ing, the superior intelligence, of those five letters so arranged. (348-9)

It is ironically appropriate that Emma should be duped at her own game of quick perception, trapped by her own imagina-tion. When Knightley, anxious to protect Emma from herself, suggests that she may be deceived regarding Frank Churchill, Emma replies in terms applicable only to herself.

> "Oh! you amuse me excessively. I am delighted to find that you can vouchsafe to let your *imagination* wander—but it will not do—very sorry to check you in your first essay—but indeed

it will not do. There is no admiration between them, I do assure you; and the *appearances* which have caught you, have
arisen from some peculiar circumstances—feelings rather of a
totally different nature:—it is impossible exactly to explain:—
there is a good deal of nonsense in it—but the part which is
capable of being communicated, which is *sense*, is, that they are
as far from any attachment or admiration for one another, as
any two beings in the world can be." (350–51; italics mine)

In the third stage of her education Emma, who knows "the
limitations of her own powers" at the pianoforte "too well to
attempt more than she could perform with credit" (227), also
discovers the limitations of her judgment and comes to recognize the distorting power of her egoistic imagination. As
she gradually awakens to her love for Mr. Knightley he passes
through the roles of father, brother, and finally lover, each
new role gathering to itself the functions of the previous one.
At first Emma is not consciously aware of her affection for
Knightley, and it finds disguised expression in her conviction
that he must never marry for the sake of his friends and family.

> Her objections to Mr. Knightley's marrying did not in the least
> subside. She could see nothing but evil in it. It would be a
> great disappointment to Mr. John Knightley; consequently to
> Isabella. A real injury to the children—a most mortifying
> change, and material loss to them all;—a very great deduction
> from her father's daily comfort—and, as to herself, she could
> not at all endure the idea of Jane Fairfax at Donwell Abbey.
> A Mrs. Knightley for them all to give way to!—No—Mr.
> Knightley must never marry. Little Henry must remain the
> heir of Donwell. (227–8)

Later the belief that Knightley "must never marry" contributes
to her mistaken estimate of Harriet's affections. And when
Emma makes her gesture of amends toward Jane Fairfax, only

to be rebuffed, we have a clear sign of her growing dependence on Knightley's judgment: "she had the consolation . . . of being able to say to herself, that could Mr. Knightley have been privy to all her attempts of assisting Jane Fairfax, could he even have seen into her heart, he would not, on this occasion, have found anything to reprove" (391).

From the beginning of the novel we are aware that Knightley speaks not only for the author, but for Emma's heart, for the natural charity which is the source of her charm. This is why Knightley's stern reprimand to Emma, after she has thoughtlessly insulted Miss Bates during the expedition to Box Hill, strikes with such force; it awakens part of herself, and comes as the voice of her own conscience. Thus it is natural and appropriate that Emma's recognition of her love for Knightley and her discovery of the deceptions she has played on herself should come together. When Harriet confesses that she cares for Mr. Knightley, and has reason to believe that he returns her affection, Emma's sudden awareness that "Mr. Knightley must marry no one but herself" is followed by recognition of all her past follies.

> Her own conduct, as well as her own heart, was before her in the same few minutes. She saw it all with a clearness which had never blessed her before. How improperly had she been acting by Harriet! How inconsiderate, how indelicate, how irrational, how unfeeling had been her conduct! What blindness, what madness, had led her on! (408)

Tormented by the thought that she has lost all hope of Knightley's love, Emma soon acknowledges the dangers of treating life as a work of the imagination.

> How to understand the deceptions she had been thus practising on herself, and living under!—The blunders, the blindness of

her own head and heart!—she sat still, she walked about, she tried her own room, she tried the shrubbery—in every place, every posture, she perceived that she had acted most weakly; that she had been imposed on by others in a most mortifying degree; that she had been imposing on herself in a degree yet more mortifying; that she was wretched, and should probably find this day but the beginning of wretchedness. . . .

With insufferable vanity had she believed herself in the secret of everybody's feelings; with unpardonable arrogance proposed to arrange everybody's destiny. She was proved to have been universally mistaken; and she had not quite done nothing—for she had done mischief (411–13)

But, of course, Emma Woodhouse is soon redeemed from wretchedness, and the mischief she has done causes only temporary pain. *Emma* concludes with happiness and reconciliation, and there is nothing forced or sentimental in this conclusion. Jane Austen's view of the world is essentially comic, and like all comic writers she cleaves to a norm of social behavior, a balance of opposing forces which finds in *Emma* its most persuasive expression. Jane Austen knows the desire of the will to assert its individuality, but she also knows that the identity of the self is a social fact. She believes that only those with imagination can explore the full range of life's possibilities, yet like Dr. Johnson she fears "that hunger of imagination which preys incessantly upon life." The beauty of *Emma* lies in the fact that Knightley is a realistic figure, not a fictional paragon, and that in accepting him Emma is embracing a social identity which harmonizes with the self of her best imagination. Here the similarity with the ending of *Pride and Prejudice* is obvious, but the differences may be more important. The two novels are separated by less than twenty years in their origins, but the social distance seems much greater. Frank Churchill's dubious behavior is harder to comprehend than Wickham's simple hypocrisies; indeed, the entire milieu of *Emma* strikes us as far more complex, more "modern," than that of *Pride and Prejudice*. Emma's desire to dominate and control, to impose her fictions upon life, is more complicated and perverse than Elizabeth Bennet's pride of judgment. In reading *Emma* we are acutely aware of the disasters that might have been, and we think not only of the heroine's predecessors in Jane Austen's fiction but of her spiritual descendants who will confront a world which can offer them no satisfying social identity.

So far we have been speaking of the novel in terms of theme and idea, but of all Jane Austen's novels *Emma* yields least readily to generalized discussion. This is, of course, a mark of the novel's greatness. Many of the earlier works can be reduced to a scheme without grave injury (I am thinking here especially of *Sense and Sensibility*); we acknowledge the wit and richness of observation that went into the making of these works, but at the same time we do not hesitate to formulate their themes in abstract language. With *Emma*, however, Jane Austen has achieved such a fine consistency of form that any critical approach seems woefully self-limiting. Here the external demands of drama have been reconciled with a growing concern for the dynamics of character, for psychological exposition, with the result that the novel achieves a unity of effect new to English fiction. Richardson had sought, most successfully in *Clarissa*, to create a form where "not one Digression, not one Episode, not one Reflection" is introduced but what it "arises naturally from the Subject, and makes for it, and [carries] it on," [8] but he never mastered the economy of expression demanded by such a nervous form. We have seen that Jane Austen's aim, from her *Juvenilia* onwards, was fixed on organic unity in the novel, and with *Emma* this aim was realized. The disparity between the actual effects of *Emma* and the descriptive vocabulary of contemporary criticism of fiction seems almost absurd, and if we seek for a critical view-point that will do justice to *Emma* we must look to the later nineteenth century, when Romantic theories of organic unity were finally applied to fiction. In "The Art of Fiction" Henry James provides us with a passage which might be taken as a motto for any study of *Emma*:

> I cannot imagine composition existing in a series of blocks, nor conceive, in any novel worth discussing at all, of a passage of description that is not in its intention narrative, a passage of dialogue that is not in its intention descriptive, a touch of truth of any sort that does not partake of the nature of incident, or an incident that derives its interest from any other source than the general and only source of the success of a work of art—that of being illustrative. A novel is a living thing, all one and con-tinuous, like any other organism, and in proportion as it lives will it be found, I think, that in each of the parts there is some-thing of each of the other parts. The critic who over the close texture of a finished work shall pretend to trace a geography of items will mark some frontiers as artificial, I fear, as any that have been known to history. . . . What is character but the determination of incident? What is incident but the illustration of character? What is either a picture or a novel that is *not* of character? What else do we seek in it and find in it? It is an incident for a woman to stand up with her hand resting on a table and look out at you in a certain way; or if it be not an incident I think it will be hard to say what it is. At the same time it is an expression of character. If you say you don't see it (character in *that—allons donc!*), this is exactly what the artist who has reasons of his own for thinking he *does* see it under-takes to show you.[9]

The "close texture" of *Emma* depends, first and last, on the intriguing consciousness of Emma Woodhouse. Emma is the center of the novel's world, and most of the action is seen through her eyes. As early as the *Juvenilia* Jane Austen had been experimenting with this method, and in *The Watsons* she began to use it on a large scale. But the treatment of Emma Woodhouse differs from earlier uses of the method in its subtlety and consistency. Because the growth of Emma's personality is the subject of the novel, we must experience her reactions to every incident. We soon become accustomed to an easy movement in and out of Emma's mind, such as is found in the following passage from Chapter III.

Harriet Smith was the natural daughter of somebody. Somebody had placed her, several years back, at Mrs. Goddard's school, and somebody had lately raised her from the condition of scholar to that of parlour-boarder. This was all that was generally known of her history. She had no visible friends but what had been acquired at Highbury, and was now just returned from a long visit in the country to some young ladies who had been at school there with her.

She was a very pretty girl, and her beauty happened to be of a sort which Emma particularly admired. She was short, plump and fair, with a fine bloom, blue eyes, light hair, regular features, and a look of great sweetness; and before the end of the evening, Emma was as much pleased with her manners as her person, and quite determined to continue the acquaintance.

She was not struck by anything remarkably clever in Miss Smith's conversation, but she found her altogether very engaging—not inconveniently shy, not unwilling to talk—and yet so far from pushing, shewing so proper and becoming a deference, seeming so pleasantly grateful for being admitted to Hartfield, and so artlessly impressed by the appearance of everything in so superior a style to what she had been used to, that she must have good sense and deserve encouragement. . . . *She* would notice her; she would improve her; she would detach her from her bad acquaintance, and introduce her into good society; she would form her opinions and her manners. It would be an interesting, and certainly a very kind undertaking; highly becoming her own situation in life, her leisure, and powers. (22–4)

In the first paragraph of this quotation Jane Austen is assuming the familiar role of self-effacing, reliable commentator, telling us what is "generally known" of Harriet's history. Then, in the second paragraph, we move to Emma's special viewpoint, and the third paragraph is given over completely to Emma's reactions. This does not mean that Jane Austen has relinquished control; the language clearly implies that Emma finds Harriet engaging because she is malleable, and because the role of "improver" appeals to Emma's vanity. But these qualifications must be expressed indirectly, so as not to break the illusion that we are viewing Harriet through Emma's eyes.

Basically, information comes to us in *Emma* from three sources: dramatic action and dialogue, expositions of Emma's thoughts and reactions, and direct summary of what is generally known and believed. The novel proceeds by a rhythmic alternation between what Henry James called "picture" and "scene": [10] the "pictures," expository passages which record Emma's thoughts and feelings, acquaint us with her personality and chart its development, while the dramatic scenes establish our hold on objective reality and furnish the materials for Emma's reflections. The key to success with this method of presentation lies in constant interaction between external and internal reality, so that we gain a double sense of dramatic events and their interpretation by an individual consciousness. Chapters XV and XVI provide a fine example of this interaction. Chapter XV is essentially dramatic: it opens in the Westons' drawing-room, with Emma vexed over Mr. Elton's "pretence" of being in love with her; continues through the discovery of snow, Mr. Woodhouse's nervousness, and the decision to return home; and culminates with Mr. Elton's violent proposal to Emma in the carriage. Most of the chapter is given over to dialogue or summary of dialogue, and the few excursions into individual reactions do not go far beyond what would be portrayed on the stage by gesture or expression. Then, in the next chapter, we are wholly within Emma's consciousness:

> The hair was curled, and the maid sent away, and Emma sat down to think and be miserable.—It was a wretched business, indeed!—Such an overthrow of every thing she had been wishing for!—Such a development of every thing most unwelcome! —Such a blow for Harriet!—That was the worst of all. Every part of it brought pain and humiliation, of some sort or other; but, compared with the evil to Harriet, all was light; and she would gladly have submitted to feel yet more mistaken—more in error—more disgraced by mis-judgment, than she actually was, could the effects of her blunders have been confined to herself. (134)

Throughout this chapter Emma indulges in a dialogue with herself, until the dramatic developments of the previous episode have become a part of her sensibility. And as she rehearses these developments we realize that Emma's view of "what happens" is, to Jane Austen, more important than the events themselves; the affairs of "3 or 4 Families in a Country Village" [11] have become part of some universal psychology.

The characteristic rhythm of *Emma* is one of approach and withdrawal, an external confrontation of wills followed by personal reassessment. Emma is the commanding center of this design, but this does not mean that her point-of-view is to be ours. Jane Austen does not intend that our vision should be in any way affected by Emma's blindness. There is a constant ironic qualification of the heroine, much of it dependent upon the language used to record Emma's reactions; in the passage from Chapter III discussed earlier, the repeated use of the personal pronoun underscores the selfish nature of Emma's interest in Harriet Smith. But these local ironies and verbal qualifications must be directed and organized if we are to gain a clear impression of Emma's self-delusion, and Wayne Booth is surely right when he maintains that we are prepared for them by the opening chapter, in which the author labels Knightley as a "sensible man" and states that "the real evils indeed of Emma's situation were the power of having rather too much her own way, and a disposition to think a little too well of herself." [12] This confident beginning, so different from the obliquity of the typical modern novel, testifies to Jane Austen's sure control over the axioms of her created world. But it is equally important to note the discretion with which Jane Austen uses her right to judge character and assert norms of behavior. Her authority is quickly vested in Mr. Knightley, and by the end of the fifth chapter we have complete faith in his judgment. As the novel progresses the author seems more and more willing to speak as impersonal historian, an authority on what is "generally known"; explicit moral comment becomes increasingly the province of Mr. Knightley, whose position within the story enhances its force.

There is nothing doctrinaire in Jane Austen's use of Emma as a commanding center for the novel; she does not hesitate to introduce scenes and dialogues from which Emma is absent. Chapter V, for example, is entirely devoted to a conversation between Mr. Knightley and Mrs. Weston which confirms our impression that Knightley is the custodian of Jane Austen's judgment. The opening of the chapter sets its judicial tone:

> "I do not know what your opinion may be, Mrs. Weston," said Mr. Knightley, "of this great intimacy between Emma and Harriet Smith, but I think it a bad thing."
> "A bad thing! Do you really think it a bad thing?—why so?"
> "I think they will neither of them do the other any good."
> (36)

Another extended departure from Emma's consciousness occurs in that scene from the third volume where Frank Churchill nearly reveals his secret correspondence with Jane

Fairfax; here we are allowed to view the action through Knightley's eyes, presumably because Jane Austen felt that a precise knowledge of Frank Churchill's duplicity was needed at this point to underscore Emma's self-deception. In both of these chapters we have no sense that the novel's point-of-view has been violated, even though Emma is temporarily placed to one side of the stage. This is partly because she is always the subject of action and dialogue; even when she is absent the conversation turns upon her behavior. But, more importantly, it is because Jane Austen has consistently maintained a point-of-view that places Emma in perspective; we are accustomed to viewing her objectively as well as through her inner life. By allowing us to share Emma's inner life without being limited by it, Jane Austen has avoided that dichotomy between the sympathetic imagination and critical judgment which runs through the earlier novels. The very form of *Emma* makes such a separation irrelevant. By placing Emma's fine and interesting mind at the center of the novel Jane Austen assured herself of our sympathy, since we experience the life of Highbury through Emma's consciousness; but at the same time she made certain that we would understand and criticize every aspect of Emma's self-deception by establishing a context of ironic qualifications and explicit judgments. Without this framework of implied and explicit criticism *Emma* would be a provincial tale, rich in particular observation but limited in significance. We appreciate the largeness of Emma's spirit precisely because we know her social and psychological errors, and are able to relate them to a world beyond the novel. Thus we can say that the general form of *Emma* reflects the novel's deepest meaning, reminding us that freedom is dependent upon a recognition of limitations.

VI

NEW LANDSCAPES

Persuasion and *Sanditon*

As we seek to define the special qualities of Jane Austen's late work our attention is inevitably drawn to the new importance she gives to natural landscapes. In the earlier fiction we visualize the characters against a man-made landscape; when the setting is not a drawing-room or ball-room it tends to be the civilized nature of eighteenth-century gardens and paintings. Trees and grass and hills are there, but they are drawn from the repertory of the picturesque, and belong in their small way to what Kenneth Clark has called the "landscape of fantasy." [1] Nature is contemplated with Gilpin and the "improvers" in mind; the landscape is described and criticized as if it were a work of art. Although the young Jane Austen delighted in ridiculing the "sublime" nature of Gothic fiction, with its rhetorical imitations of Salvator Rosa, we know from her brother Henry that she had been "enamoured of Gilpin on the Picturesque" at an early age. [2] It is not surprising, then, that Elizabeth Bennet's interest in the Lake Country is that of the amateur artist, or that she views Pemberley Woods with an eye to picturesque stage-effects. But with *Mansfield Park* a new feeling for external nature begins to emerge, and in *Emma* we find an expressive use of landscape that contrasts sharply with the descriptions of the early fiction. The course of Emma Woodhouse's life is subtly related to the cycle of the seasons: Mr. Elton's distressing proposal takes place against the background of a dark and snowy December evening, while Knightley's confession of love occurs on a delightful day in July.[3] The chapter in which Jane Austen brings Emma and Mr. Knightley together opens with a descriptive passage that foreshadows the human changes:

> The weather continued much the same [a cold stormy rain] all the following morning; and the same loneliness, and the same melancholy, seemed to reign at Hartfield—but in the afternoon it cleared; the wind changed into a softer quarter; the clouds were carried off; the sun appeared; it was summer again. With all the eagerness which such a transition gives, Emma resolved to be out of doors as soon as possible. Never had the exquisite sight, smell, sensation of nature, tranquil, warm, and brilliant after a storm, been more attractive to her. (424)

This symbolic use of the natural setting involves a "sensation of nature" foreign to the early works, and we find the sensation intensified in *Persuasion,* where Anne Elliot's melancholy and "early loss of bloom" (28) are continuously presented through the imagery of autumn. In the following description of a November walk Anne's feeling for the landscape harmonizes with the emotions prompted by the dialogue.

> Her *pleasure* in the walk must arise from the exercise and the day, from the view of the last smiles of the year upon the tawny leaves and withered hedges, and from repeating to herself some few of the thousand poetical descriptions extant of autumn, that season of peculiar and inexhaustible influence on the mind of taste and tenderness . . . After one of the many praises of

the day, which were continually bursting forth, Captain Wentworth added,

"What glorious weather for the Admiral and my sister! They
meant to take a long drive this morning; perhaps we may hail
them from some of these hills. They talked of coming into this
side of the country. I wonder whereabouts they will upset
to-day. Oh! it does happen very often, I assure you—but my
sister makes nothing of it—she would as lieve be tossed out as
not."

"Ah! You make the most of it, I know," cried Louisa, "but if
it were really so, I should do just the same in her place. If I
loved a man, as she loves the Admiral, I would be always with
him, nothing should ever separate us, and I would rather be
overturned by him, than driven safely by anybody else."

It was spoken with enthusiasm.

"Had you?" cried he, catching the same tone; "I honour you!"
And there was silence between them for a little while.

Anne could not immediately fall into a quotation again. The
sweet scenes of autumn were for a while put by—unless some
tender sonnet, fraught with the apt analogy of the declining
year, with declining happiness, and the images of youth and
hope, and spring, all gone together, blessed her memory. She
roused herself to say, as they struck by order into another path,
"Is not this one of the ways to Winthrop?" But nobody heard,
or, at least, nobody answered her.

Winthrop, however, or its environs—for young men are,
sometimes, to be met with, strolling about near home, was their
destination; and after another half mile of gradual ascent
through large enclosures, where the ploughs at work, and the
fresh-made path spoke the farmer, counteracting the sweets of
poetical despondence, and meaning to have spring again, they
gained the summit of the most considerable hill, which parted
Uppercross and Winthrop, and soon commanded a full view of
the latter, at the foot of the hill on the other side. (84–5)

The effects of this passage are new to Jane Austen's art.
Anne's consciousness is the focus of the scene, and our interest

is in her reactions, but these reactions are expressed more through descriptive details than through exposition. The tone of the landscape controls the passage: Anne's regret is imaged in the autumn scene, while the reminder of spring—in immediate context a sad reminder—may also be read as a hint of future happiness. This "poetic" reliance on natural landscape is even more striking in *Sanditon*, the fragmentary work that closes Jane Austen's career. As E. M. Forster has observed, the town of Sanditon is "not like Lyme or Highbury or Northanger or the other places that provide scenes or titles to past novels. It exists in itself and for itself. Character-drawing, incident, and wit are on the decline, but topography comes to the front, and is screwed much deeper than usual into the story." [4]

The sources of this new quality in Jane Austen's fiction must have been complex, but one point seems obvious. More than has been generally realized or acknowledged, she was influenced by the Romantic poetry of the early nineteenth century. *Persuasion* and *Sanditon* contain a number of references to contemporary poets, to Byron, Wordsworth, and especially Scott. And although Jane Austen's explicit use of these authors may be for the purposes of satire, her late prose reflects their influence. Nature has ceased to be a mere backdrop; landscape is a structure of feeling which can express, and also modify, the minds of those who view it. In their quiet and restrained fashion, Jane Austen's last works are part of the new movement in English literature. She has learned that the natural setting can convey, more surely than any abstract vocabulary, the movements of an individual imagination.

This method for expressing individual moods was needed in *Persuasion*, for in her work on this novel Jane Austen set herself a new problem of communication. To put it quite simply, the sense of community has disappeared, and the heroine finds herself terribly alone. Anne Elliot has no trustworthy

confidante, no Jane Bennet, or Mrs. Weston, or Mr. Knightley. The sympathetic brothers, sisters, and fathers of the earlier
novels have disappeared; Lady Russell cannot comprehend
Anne Elliot, and the heroine is locked in the world of her own
consciousness. Anne's need is as much communication as it is
love, and in spite of the happy ending the deepest impression
we carry away from *Persuasion* is one of human isolation.
D. H. Lawrence's well-known attack on Jane Austen is
directly relevant here:

> The sense of isolation, followed by the sense of menace and
> of fear, is bound to arise as the feeling of oneness and com-
> munity with our fellow-men declines, and the feeling of indi-
> vidualism and personality, which is existence in isolation, in-
> creases. . . . Class-hate and class-consciousness are only a sign
> that the old togetherness, the old blood-warmth has collapsed,
> and every man is really aware of himself in apartness. . . . In
> the old England, the curious blood-connections held the classes
> together. The squires might be arrogant, violent, bullying and
> unjust, yet in some ways they were at one with the people, part
> of the same blood-stream. We feel it in Defoe or Fielding. And
> then, in the mean Jane Austen, it is gone. Already this old
> maid typifies "personality" instead of character, the sharp know-
> ing in apartness instead of knowing in togetherness . . .[5]

After we have discounted Lawrence's masculine antagonism
toward Jane Austen, and his characteristic identification of
art with life, we are left with a penetrating statement of the
essential themes in *Persuasion*. In a sense, *Persuasion* begins
where the other novels end: Anne knows her own heart, and is
not deluded about herself. Yet she is isolated, haunted by a
"sense of menace and fear"; she knows only in "apartness."
Her despair is that of the modern "personality," forced to live
within itself. We may attribute this quality in *Persuasion* to
the frustrations of Jane Austen's middle-age (for the first time

there is no fictional counterpart to Cassandra), but such biographical speculations are of limited usefulness. It is better to
view *Persuasion* as a final variation on one of Jane Austen's
most persistent themes, the perils of the free spirit in its search
for social identity. Here this theme is given its darkest treatment. Anne Elliot is denied the retreat into obsolete manners
symbolized by Mansfield Park, just as she is cut off from the
fatherly advice of a Mr. Knightley. The social world of *Persuasion* seems cruelly unhelpful, and one must conclude that Jane
Austen is expressing in the novel her alarm at contemporary
changes in English manners. In spite of the final marriage and
the brave flourishes of the last chapter, *Persuasion* looks forward to a society where the burdens of personality must be
borne without a compensating "feeling of oneness and community." The familiar world of the nineteenth-century novel
is at hand.

The technical difficulties Jane Austen faced in her work on
Persuasion were formidable, the direct result of her chosen
subject. The drama of self-deception and self-recognition
which holds our interest in the earlier novels is almost totally
absent from *Persuasion*, and without it the field for irony is
greatly reduced. The personality of Anne Elliot must carry all
our interest without the benefit of dramatic irony, and to
accomplish this Jane Austen has made Anne's point-of-view
that of the reader. Everything depends on our sympathy with
Anne, and our interest in her fate. The contrast between this
narrative method and that of *Emma* is highly significant. Since
Emma Woodhouse does not know her own mind, we soon
learn that we cannot identify our vision with hers; and although most of the action of *Emma* is seen through the heroine's eyes Jane Austen has supplied us with glimpses into
other minds, and with reliable commentary from herself and
Knightley. But, as Wayne Booth has pointed out, the only
significant break in "angle of vision" between the first and last

chapters of *Persuasion* occurs in the scene where Anne meets Captain Wentworth for the first time in many years. The sympathetic reader is likely to assume that he is still in love with Anne. As Booth says,

> All the conventions of art favor such a belief: the emphasis is clearly on Anne and her unhappiness; the lover has returned; we have only to wait, perhaps with some tedium, for the inevitable outcome. Anne learns (chap. vii) that he has spoken of her as so altered "he should not have known her again." "These were words which could not but dwell with her. Yet she soon began to rejoice that she had heard them. They were of sobering tendency; they allayed agitation; they composed, and consequently must make her happier." And suddenly we enter Wentworth's mind for one time only: "Frederick Wentworth had used such words, or something like them, but without an idea that they would be carried round to her. He had thought her wretchedly altered, and, in the first moment of appeal, had spoken as he felt. He had not forgiven Anne Elliot. She had used him ill"—and so he goes on, for five more paragraphs. The necessary point, the fact that Frederick believes himself to be indifferent, has been made, and it could not have been made without some kind of shift from Anne's consciousness.[6]

This isolated excursion into the mind of another character does not disturb us, since in the opening chapter the author has presented the situation and characters to us in her own voice; but I doubt if it has convinced many readers. We know that Wentworth's love will be easily reawakened, and our real interest lies in Anne's struggle to overcome the barriers of social isolation and communicate with the man she once knew so well. It is for this reason that Jane Austen presents almost all the action from her point-of-view.

Of the surviving Austen manuscripts, the two "canceled" chapters of *Persuasion* reveal the most about her artistic methods. On 18 July 1816 she wrote "Finis" at the end of the second volume, which then contained eleven chapters; but the handling of the reconciliation scene still did not satisfy her, and during the next two weeks or so she recast the tenth chapter into the present tenth and eleventh chapters, recopying the last chapter (now the twelfth) with verbal corrections. In his separate edition of the two original chapters R. W. Chapman has recorded manuscript corrections and variants from the posthumous first edition,[7] and a study of these corrections and additions reveals the same care for phrasing and rhythm we discovered in the revisions of *The Watsons*. Presumably more verbal changes would have been made in the final preparation for the press, if Jane Austen had lived. But these small changes are less illuminating than the structural changes which occurred when the original Chapter X was transformed into the present Chapters X and XI. By comparing the two versions we can gain a new sense of Jane Austen's skill in construction, and a feeling for the artistic ideals that governed her work on *Persuasion*.

In the ninth chapter of the second volume Anne pays her visit to Mrs. Smith at Westgate-buildings, in the course of which she learns of Mr. Elliot's true character. This revelation is the subject of Anne's thoughts at the beginning of the original Chapter X. She is walking down Gay Street, considering the implications of her new knowledge, when she encounters Admiral Croft. His home is only a few steps away, and Anne is persuaded—much against her wishes—to enter and speak to Mrs. Croft. It is only when she has reached the threshold of the drawing room that Anne is casually informed, "there is nobody but Frederick here." As soon as she is confronted with Captain Wentworth, Admiral Croft draws him outside the door and begins a conversation in which Anne hears "her own name & *Kellynch*" mentioned repeatedly. Captain Wentworth re-enters the room, and, after a moment of embarrassment, begins to speak on the Admiral's behalf.

"The Adm¹, Madam, was this morning confidently informed that you were—upon my word I am quite at a loss, ashamed—(breathing & speaking quick)—the awkwardness of *giving* Information of this sort to one of the Parties—You can be at no loss to understand me—It was very confidently said that Mʳ Elliot—that everything was settled in the family for an Union between Mʳ Elliot—& yourself. It was added that you were to live at Kellynch—that Kellynch was to be given up. This, the Admiral knew could not be correct—But it occurred to him that it might be the *wish* of the Parties—And my commission from him Madam, is to say, that if the Family wish is such, his Lease of Kellynch shall be cancel'd . . ." [8]

Falteringly, Anne informs Wentworth that the Admiral has been misinformed; and, encouraged by her denial and countenance, the Captain confesses his love.

Her Countenance did not discourage.—It was a silent, but a very powerful Dialogue;—on his side, Supplication, on her's acceptance.—Still, a little nearer—and a hand taken and pressed—and "Anne, my own dear Anne!"—bursting forth in the fullness of exquisite feeling—and all Suspense & Indecision were over. [9]

The rest of the canceled chapter is given over to Wentworth's account of his own feelings and behavior during their separation.

It is easy to see why Jane Austen was dissatisfied with this handling of the reconciliation. The climax comes so close on the heels of Anne's visit to Mrs. Smith that we are taken by surprise; the two critical scenes are so close together that they detract from each other. Furthermore, Anne's difficulties with her family have almost been forgotten. In rewriting the chapter Jane Austen retained a good portion of Wentworth's account of his own feelings; this needed little revision. But she completely altered the circumstances of the reconciliation, and separated it from the visit to Westgate-buildings by a new chapter devoted to Anne's family.

In the final version of the novel Chapter X opens with Anne returning home after her visit to Mrs. Smith. She is exposed to the humiliating behavior of Elizabeth and Mrs. Clay; Mr. Elliot enters, and is treated coldly by Anne. We then shift to the next day; Anne is preparing to visit Lady Russell and tell her of Mr. Elliot's true nature, when the Musgroves suddenly arrive. The visit to Lady Russell is postponed, and Anne joins her friends of the past autumn at the White Hart. Captain Wentworth arrives, and Anne must shortly suffer another meeting between the Captain and her family. Mr. Elliot, supposedly out of town, is glimpsed in the company of Mrs. Clay. The next day (Chapter XI) Anne returns to the White Hart and finds that Captain Wentworth has already arrived. He soon calls for writing materials and begins a letter. Encouraged by the events of the previous day and the tenor of her conversation with Captain Harville, which he overhears, Wentworth composes a hasty love letter and contrives to place it in Anne's hands. The reconciliation has been accomplished, and when they meet a short time later Wentworth launches into an explanation of his past feelings and actions.

Even this crude summary of the changes made in revision can show the complexity of Jane Austen's aims and the sureness of her execution. The new tenth chapter reasserts Anne's isolation, and—through the momentary revelation of the affair between Mr. Elliot and Mrs. Clay—confirms the impressions of the previous chapter. By decelerating the pace of events Jane Austen has given full weight to Mr. Elliot's duplicity, and prepared us for the understanding between Anne and Captain Wentworth. In this connection the indirect appeal by letter seems far superior to the direct confrontation of the earlier version; it emphasizes that difficulty of communication which has been the novel's major theme. Significantly, the final version sustains the internal point-of-view, allowing us to follow the turns of Anne's mind, while the shorter draft had threatened to break this psychological consistency and collapse into straight summary. It is fortunate that this fine example of Jane Austen's structural revisions has survived, since it gives us a clear sense of the rigorous self-criticism and technical control which went into the making of her mature novels.

The unfinished *Sanditon*, which was abandoned four months before Jane Austen's death, has been a puzzle and challenge to critics of her fiction. Its final shape can hardly be discerned: as Mary Lascelles has said, none of Jane Austen's other works, "if broken off short at the eleventh chapter, [would] have left us in such uncertainty as to the way in which it was going to develop." [10] The state of Jane Austen's health seems to have had a decisive effect on the fragment's tone; her other works are filled with hypochondriacs (hypochondria usually signifying a retreat from reality), but in *Sanditon* the ironic attack on complacent invalidism is so persistent and intense that it must be connected with the onset of her final illness. To the end of her career Jane Austen used irony as an instrument of self-criticism.

But the comedy of *Sanditon* seems far removed from that of *Emma* or *Pride and Prejudice*. In fact, with its broad burlesques of manners and its attacks on "excessive sensibility," *Sanditon* harks back to the comic methods of the *Juvenilia*. Sir Edward Denham's raptures remind us of *Love and Freindship,* although the literary examples are now drawn from the new poetry instead of the novels of sensibility.

"Do you remember, said he, Scott's beautiful Lines on the Sea?—Oh! what a description they convey!—They are never out

of my Thoughts when I walk here.—That Man who can read
them unmoved must have the nerves of an Assassin!—Heaven
defend me from meeting such a Man un-armed."—"What description do you mean?—said Charlotte. I remember none at this
moment, of the Sea, in either of Scott's Poems."—"Do not you
indeed?—Nor can I exactly recall the beginning at this moment
—But—you cannot have forgotten his description of Woman.—

"Oh! Woman in our Hours of Ease—"

Delicious! Delicious!—Had he written nothing more, he w^d
have been Immortal. And then again, that unequalled, unri-
valled address to Parental affection—

"Some feelings are to Mortals given
With less of Earth in them than Heaven" &c

But while we are on the subject of Poetry, what think you
Miss H. of Burns Lines to his Mary?—Oh! there is Pathos to
madden one!—If ever there was a Man who *felt*, it was Burns.
—Montgomery has all the Fire of Poetry, Wordsworth has the
true soul of it—Campbell in his pleasures of Hope has touched
the extreme of our Sensations . . . But Burns is always on
fire.—His Soul was the Altar in which lovely Woman sat en-
shrined, his Spirit truly breathed the immortal Incence which
is her Due.—" "I have read several of Burn's Poems with great
delight, said Charlotte as soon as she had time to speak, but I
am not poetic enough to separate a Man's Poetry entirely from
his Character;—& poor Burns's known Irregularities, greatly
interrupt my enjoyment of his Lines." (396–8) [11]

This is the familiar debate between Sensibility and Sense, re-
hearsed in terms of a new generation. Sir Edward, who is
"very much addicted to all the newest-fashioned hard words"
(398), is a Man of Feeling who thrives on Romantic verse.
His comments on novel-reading lead us back to the parodies
of the *Juvenilia:*

"I am no indiscriminate Novel-Reader. The mere Trash of the common Circulating Library, I hold in the highest contempt. You will never hear me advocating those puerile Emanations which detail nothing but discordant Principles incapable of Amalgamation, or those vapid tissues of ordinary Occurrences from which no useful Deductions can be drawn.—In vain may we put them into a literary Alembic;—we distil nothing which can add to Science.—You understand me I am sure?" "I am not quite certain that I do.—[said Charlotte] But if you will describe the sort of Novels which you *do* approve, I dare say it will give me a clearer idea." "Most willingly, Fair Questioner. —The Novels which I approve are such as display Human Nature with Grandeur—such as shew her in the Sublimities of intense Feeling—such as exhibit the progress of strong Passion from the first Germ of incipient Susceptibility to the utmost Energies of Reason half-dethroned . . ." (403)

This absurd mixture of novel-jargon and phrases culled from the new quarterlies stands in sharp contrast to the realistic dialogues of the late novels, and we are faced with the question: why did Jane Austen return to parody and burlesque in the composition of *Sanditon*?

One answer is that she had never really abandoned these devices as a source of personal delight and family entertainment; the spirit of the *Juvenilia* lived on in her letters. But it would be more exact to say that this spirit suffered a temporary diminution during her difficult middle life, only to be revived with enthusiasm sometime around 1813. The shift in mood which we experience when we move from *Mansfield Park* to *Emma,* the sense of liberation, is mirrored in the letters; after 1813 they sparkle with parody and playfulness. In March 1814 Jane Austen read Barrett's *The Heroine,* a burlesque of the Radcliffean romances, and reported to Cassandra that she was "very much amused by it." [12] Soon she would be interested enough in burlesque and parody to consider publishing the long-neglected *Northanger Abbey*. A major cause of this revival of interest may have been the literary efforts of the young Austens, especially James's daughter Anna. The juvenile writing of Anna must have reminded Jane Austen of her own early efforts, and she entered with enthusiasm into Anna's amusing ridicule of "novels from the circulating library at Alton." [13] Anna and her aunt read together "a most tiresome novel, in eight volumes, by a Mrs. Hunter, containing story within story, and in which the heroine was always in floods of tears"; [14] and it was this absurd romance which prompted the following mock-letter.

Miss Jane Austen begs her best Thanks may be conveyed to Mrs Hunter of Norwich for the thread paper which she has been so kind as to send her by Mr Austen, and which will always be very valuable on account of the spirited sketches (made it is supposed by Nicholson or Glover) of those most interesting spots Tarefield Hall, the Mill & above all else Tomb of Howards wife of the faithful representation of which Miss Jane Austen is undoubtedly a good judge having spent so many summers at Tarefield Abbey the delighted guest of the worthy Mrs Wilson.—It is impossible for any likeness to be more complete. Miss J. A.'s tears have flowed over each sweet sketch in such a way as would do Mrs Hs heart good to see . . .

Miss J. A. cannot close this small Epitome of the miniature of an abridgement of her Thanks & admiration without expressing her sincere hopes that M^{rs} H is provided with a more safe conveyance to London than Alton can now boast—as the Car of Falkenstein which was the pride of that Town was overturned within the last ten days.[15]

This combination of literary parody and a family joke points forward to the high-spirited *Plan of a Novel*, composed in 1815–16. The Reverend J. S. Clarke, librarian to the Prince Regent, had suggested that Jane Austen might wish "to delineate in some future Work the Habits of Life and Character and enthusiasm of a Clergyman—who should pass his time between the metropolis & the Country—who should be something like Beatties Minstrel." [16] Jane Austen's reply to this extraordinary request was a modest statement that she lacked the learning necessary to do justice to such a subject; [17] the irony we read into this letter would not have existed for Mr. Clarke. But in private Jane Austen constructed a mock *Plan of a Novel, according to hints from various quarters,* in which the suggestions of Mr. Clarke, and of various friends and members of the family, are woven into a delightful burlesque of literary conventions.[18] The heroine of *Plan of a Novel,* who is "perfectly good, with much tenderness & sentiment, & not the least Wit," is often "carried away by the anti-hero, but rescued either by her Father or the Hero."

> At last, hunted out of civilized Society, denied the poor Shelter of the humblest Cottage, they [the heroine and her father] are compelled to retreat into Kamschatka where the poor Father, quite worn down, finding his end approaching, throws himself on the Ground, & after 4 or 5 hours of tender advice & parental Admonition to his miserable Child, expires in a fine burst of Literary Enthusiasm . . . Heroine inconsolable for some time —but afterwards crawls back towards her former Country—having at least 20 narrow escapes of falling into the hands of Anti-hero—& at last in the very nick of time, turning a corner to avoid him, runs into the arms of the Hero himself, who having just shaken off the scruples which fetter'd him before, was at the very moment setting off in pursuit of her.[19]

I have dwelt on this revival of burlesque and parody in Jane Austen's family life in order to demonstrate that the unfinished "Last Work" is essentially a private composition. Unlike the surviving manuscripts of *The Watsons* and the last chapters of *Persuasion, Sanditon* must be classed with the *Juvenilia* as an experiment or a private amusement. The character descriptions of *Sanditon* are cast in that abstract, Johnsonian vocabulary which Jane Austen used throughout her letters as a kind of short-hand, but which is less common in her late novels; and this would tend to confirm the tentative nature of *Sanditon*. Furthermore, the revisions on the manuscript of *Sanditon* cannot be taken as evidence that the work was recast with publication in mind; as R. W. Chapman has pointed out in his Preface to the separate edition, the corrections "are not such as could have resulted from subsequent revision of a fair copy previously made. In very many places the author has changed her mind *currente calamo;* has begun a sentence in one form and finished it in another. The number and nature of such changes create a presumption, at least, that we are dealing with a first draft." [20]

In short, it seems likely that the writing of *Sanditon* was a defense against illness and depression. The satiric treatment of hypochondria held self-pity at bay, while the revival of early burlesque methods enabled Jane Austen to recapture some of the vitality of her youth. Gone is the "autumnal" mood of *Persuasion*. The impersonal tone of *Sanditon* is a barrier against regret.

If I am correct in my assumptions about the nature of *Sanditon*, we should not criticize it in the same way as we would the major novels. Instead, we should look to *Sanditon*, as we do to any author's private communications, not for artistic effects which can only be achieved through elaborate and self-conscious construction, but for signs of the author's changing moods and new interests. And these *Sanditon* provides in abundance. First, we have the preoccupation with contemporary literature. Jane Austen had already approached this subject in *Persuasion* through her treatment of Captain Benwick.

He was evidently a young man of considerable taste in reading, though principally in poetry; and besides the persuasion of having given him at least an evening's indulgence in the discussion of subjects, which his usual companions had probably no concern in, she [Anne] had the hope of being of real use to him in some suggestions as to the duty and benefit of struggling against affliction, which had naturally grown out of their conversation. For, though shy, he did not seem reserved; it had rather the appearance of feelings glad to burst their usual restraints; and having talked of poetry, the richness of the present age, and gone through a brief comparison of opinion as to the first-rate poets, trying to ascertain whether *Marmion* or *The Lady of the Lake* were to be preferred, and how ranked the *Giaour* and *The Bride of Abydos*; and moreover, how the *Giaour* was to be pronounced, he shewed himself so intimately acquainted with all the tenderest songs of the one poet, and all the impassioned descriptions of hopeless agony of the other; he repeated, with such tremulous feeling, the various lines which imaged a broken heart, or a mind destroyed by wretchedness, and looked so entirely as if he meant to be understood, that she ventured to hope he did not always read only poetry . . . (100)

Captain Benwick promises to be a latter-day Catherine Morland, viewing the world through Romantic verse just as Catherine had viewed it through Gothic fiction. Jane Austen had learned how to present and control Catherine's illusions through her early burlesques of Gothic novels and the cult of sensibility, and we can assume that if she had lived the burlesque treatment of Sir Edward Denham would have prepared the way for further serious fiction. Just as *Persuasion* testifies to her awareness of changing social conditions, so *Sanditon* reflects her continued interest in the impact of art upon life.

Another sign provided by *Sanditon* is one we have already touched on—Jane Austen's growing concern with physical setting and the details of place. Although in 1814 she could criticize her niece Anna for giving "too many particulars of right hand & left," [21] *Sanditon* is filled with such particulars, and their treatment is so functional that the village of Sanditon possesses more reality than the characters who inhabit it. E. M. Forster has said that Sanditon "gives out an atmosphere, and also exists as a geographic and economic force." [22] We are reminded of the early *Evelyn* (*Volume the Third*), but whereas in this juvenile work the village of Evelyn is given allegorical treatment (note the overtones of the place-name), in *Sanditon* the village exists as both a realistic locale and a symbol of human illusion (it is being promoted as a "health resort"). Take for an example the following descriptive passage: I have indicated the running revisions by placing the original phrasing in brackets.

They were now approaching the Church & real village of [original] Sanditon, which stood at the foot of the [Down] Hill they were afterwards to ascend—a Hill, whose side was covered with the Woods & enclosures of Sanditon House [but whose Top was] and whose Height ended in an open Down [overlooking the Sea] where the new Build^{gs} might soon be looked for. A branch only, of the Valley, [wound] winding more obliquely towards the Sea, [giving] gave a passage to an inconsiderable Stream, & [forming] formed at its mouth, a 3^d Habitable Division, in a small cluster of Fisherman's Houses.—The village contained little more than Cottages, but the Spirit of the day had been caught, as Mr P. observed with [great pleasure] delight to Charlotte, & two or three of the best of them were smartened up with a white Curtain & "Lodgings to let"—, and farther on, in the little Green Court of an old Farm House, [were actually] two Females in elegant white were actually to be seen with their books & camp stools—and in turning the corner of the Baker's shop, the sound of a Harp might be heard [from the open] through the upper Casement.—Such sights & sounds were highly [exhilarating] Blissful to Mr P.—Not that he had any personal concern in the success of the Village itself; for considering it as too remote from the Beach, he had done nothing there—but it was a most valuable proof of the increasing fashion of the place altogether.[23]

The careful attention to topographical details evidenced in this passage gives *Sanditon* an atmosphere unique in Jane Austen's fiction. Our feeling for the place, its buildings and its weather, becomes an important part of the drama; we have a curious sense of fleshless figures moving against a realistic landscape. This is partly the result of Jane Austen's weary refusal to grapple once more with the problems of personality, but the landscape of *Sanditon* could not have been so fully realized if she had not been concerned with new effects of place and atmosphere. In the final chapter of *Sanditon* there is a scene that illuminates this new concern:

The road to Sanditon H. was a broad, handsome, planted approach, between fields, & conducting at the end of a q^r of a mile through second Gates into the Grounds, which though not extensive had all the Beauty & Respectability which an abundance of very fine Timber could give.—These Entrance Gates were so much in a corner of the Grounds or Paddock, so near one of its Boundaries, that an outside fence was at first almost pressing on the road—till an angle *here,* & a curve *there* threw them to a better distance. The Fence was a proper Park paling in excellent condition; with clusters of fine Elms, or rows of old Thorns following its line almost every where.—*Almost* must be stipulated—for there were vacant spaces—& through one of these, Charlotte as soon as they entered the Enclosure, caught a glimpse over the pales of something White & Womanish in the field on the other side;—it was something which immediately brought Miss B. into her head—& stepping to the pales, she saw indeed—& very decidedly, in spite of the Mist; Miss B—seated, not far before her, at the foot of the bank which sloped down from the outside of the Paling & which a narrow Path seemed to skirt along;—Miss Brereton seated, apparently very composedly—& Sir E. D. by her side.—They were sitting so near each other & appeared so closely engaged in gentle conversation, that Ch. instantly felt she had nothing to do but to step back again, & say not a word.—Privacy was certainly their object.—It could not but strike her rather unfavourably with regard to Clara;—but hers was a situation which must not be judged with severity.—She was glad to perceive that nothing had been discerned by Mrs Parker; If Charlotte had not been considerably the tallest of the two, Miss B.'s white ribbons might not have fallen within the ken of *her* more observant eyes. (426)

R. W. Chapman is surely right when he says of this scene that "all the items of *chiaroscuro*—the mist, the treacherous fence, the ill-defined flutter of ribbons—add up to an effect which is as clearly deliberate as it is certainly novel," [24] but the passage is more than a novel study in light-and-shade. In it the stable vantage-point of the picturesque has disappeared, and Charlotte is moving through a landscape which changes as her viewpoint changes. When the solid world of familiar objects, of trees and palings and parkland, suddenly yields to "a glimpse over the pales of something White & Womanish," Charlotte intuitively recognizes Clara Brereton; and then, as she betters her viewpoint and the outlines of the scene become clear, Charlotte's immediate impression (based upon half-conscious suspicions) is confirmed. A complex emotional experience has been expressed in visual terms, against a landscape which is charged with poetic significance. The potentialities of this method are never fully realized in Jane Austen's late work, but it is appropriate and natural that the last scene she constructed should be so pregnant with artistic possibilities. Even with the end of her life in sight Jane Austen was still exercising those critical powers which had made her artistic career a process of continuous development and discovery.

APPENDIX

Chronology of Composition

Although the chronology of Jane Austen's work after 1811 is known in some detail, there is a good deal of controversy as to the course of her earlier writing. The table printed below outlines my own view of the sequence of her artistic career; it is followed by a series of brief discussions justifying the dates I have assigned to each work.

Jane Austen's brother Henry, in his "Biographical Notice of the Author," referred to some of the novels as "the gradual performances of her previous life," and it is probable that many of the works underwent cursory revisions and retouchings of which we know nothing. Nevertheless, I am unable to accept Mrs. Leavis's theory that Jane Austen was incessantly revising her early fictions, and that most of the novels are "palimpsests through whose surface portions of earlier versions, or of other and earlier compositions quite unrelated, constantly protrude . . ." [*Scrutiny*, X (June 1941), 61–87; and X (October and January 1941–42), 114–42, 272–94]. For some telling criticisms of Mrs. Leavis's hypotheses, see Mudrick's *Jane Austen*, Appendix II, and B. C. Southam, "Mrs. Leavis and Miss Austen: the 'Critical Theory' Reconsidered," *Nineteenth Century Fiction*, XVII (June 1962), 21–32. My own objections to Mrs. Leavis's position are implicit in the discussions of individual works. In general I accept the traditional opinion that Jane Austen's artistic career divides into two periods which are separated by the disturbing years of residence in Bath and Southampton (1801–09).

I. STEVENTON, 1775–1801

c. 1788–93	*Juvenilia*
1794 or 1795	*Lady Susan* (without the Conclusion)
c. 1795	*Elinor and Marianne,* the earliest version of *Sense and Sensibility,* cast in epistolary form
October 1796–August 1797	Composition of *First Impressions,* original of *Pride and Prejudice*
November 1797	*Sense and Sensibility* begun "in its present form"
1798–99	Drafting of *Northanger Abbey* (then called *Susan,* later *Catherine*)

II. BATH AND SOUTHAMPTON, 1801–09

1803	*Susan* prepared and offered for publication
1803–04	*The Watsons* (unfinished)
c. 1805	Fair copy of *Lady Susan* (and possibly composition of the Conclusion)

III. CHAWTON, 1809–17

1809	Reawakening of interest: inquiries to the publisher concerning *Susan,* later *Northanger Abbey* (which had been sold to Crosby and Co. in 1803 but never published); scattered revisions in the *Juvenilia;* possibly a retouching of *Susan.*

1809–11	*Sense and Sensibility* revised and prepared for publication
November 1811	Publication of *Sense and Sensibility*
c. 1812	Radical revision of *Pride and Prejudice*, based on the almanacs of 1811–12
February 1811– Summer 1813	Composition of *Mansfield Park*
January 1813	Publication of *Pride and Prejudice*
May 1814	Publication of *Mansfield Park*
January 1814– March 1815	Composition of *Emma*
c. 1815	*Plan of a Novel*
December 1815	Publication of *Emma*
August 1815– August 1816	Drafting of *Persuasion*
1816	*Advertisement* to *Catherine* (later *Northanger Abbey*)
January–March 1817	Work on the fragment *Sanditon*
December 1817	Posthumous publication of *Northanger Abbey* and *Persuasion*

Juvenilia.

The dates in the *Juvenilia* (those assigned to the pieces by Jane Austen or ascertainable on the basis of the dedications) range from 1790 to 1793. Probably most of the pieces were written before Jane Austen was seventeen, and she may have begun writing as early as the age of eleven; her niece Caroline remembered that aunt Jane once advised her to cease writing until she was sixteen, and Caroline was less than twelve when this advice was given [*Memoir,* pp. 47–8]. Many of the *Juvenilia* must have been written well before their dedication dates. In general, the pieces of *Volume the First* can be dated before those in the second and third volumes. The authors of the *Life* believed [p. 57] that *Volume the Third* marked a "second stage in her literary education: when she was hesitating between burlesque and immature story-telling. . . ." The volumes of *Juve-*

nilia were a "collected edition, not the original manuscripts" [R. W. Chapman, Preface to the *Juvenilia* in *Minor Works*], and they were treasured by the family. Evidence that Jane Austen's interest in the *Juvenilia* persisted long after she had turned to other works may be found in the circumstance that a letter in *Evelyn* (*Volume the Third*) is dated "Augst 19th 1809," while in a revision of *Catharine* Hannah More's *Coelebs* (first published in 1809) was substituted for a reference to Bishop Secker on the Catechism. Presumably these late retouchings were connected with the general revival of Jane Austen's literary activity in 1809.

For a convincing discussion of the chronology of composition in *Volume the First,* see B. C. Southam's "The Manuscript of Jane Austen's Volume the First," *The Library,* Fifth Series, XVII (September 1962), 231–7.

Lady Susan.

This work survives in a fair copy made no earlier than 1805 (as witnessed by the watermarks). The authors of the *Life* believed [p. 80] that *Lady Susan* was written around 1794, and this seems quite likely. In spite of the work's complex irony and the skillful management of the epistolary form, I feel that *Lady Susan* is closely related to the more mature pieces in the *Juvenilia* (especially *Catharine,* "The Three Sisters," and "A Collection of Letters"). The fact that *Elinor and Marianne* was Jane Austen's last known use of the epistolary structure suggests a similar date for *Lady Susan.* The hasty Conclusion to the work opens with a hit at the novel-in-letters, and Mary Lascelles is probably right in her supposition that the Conclusion "was added at some time nearer to the date of the fair copy, when Jane Austen had lost patience with the device of the novel-in-letters" (Lascelles, pp. 13–14).

B. C. Southam, who has examined Jane Austen's manuscript works in great detail, agrees with this early dating of *Lady Susan.* "Internal evidence suggests that *Lady Susan* was already written by 1795. . . . The manuscript is a fair copy, the transcription of a work which, judging by its style, subject matter, and treatment, was written immediately after the last of the juvenilia, that is about 1793 or 1794. The 'Conclusion' was probably added later, perhaps at the time of transcription, sometime after 1805" ["Mrs. Leavis and Miss Austen: The 'Critical Theory' Reconsidered," *Nineteenth Century Fiction*, XVII (June 1962), 27].

Northanger Abbey.

We know from Cassandra Austen's Memorandum that "Northanger Abbey was written about the years 98 & 99" (the authors of the *Life* altered these dates to 1797–98, and subsequent critics repeated the error; B. C. Southam was the first to notice this discrepancy [see his note in the *TLS*, 12 October 1962]). One critic [C. S. Emden, "*Northanger Abbey* Re-Dated?," *Notes & Queries*, CXCV (September 1950), 407–10] has argued that the burlesque of Gothic fiction in *Northanger Abbey* was superimposed upon an earlier satire of manners and the sentimental novel dating from *c.* 1794. This is in some ways an attractive hypothesis: the sections of *Northanger Abbey* that burlesque Gothic fiction are such as might have been easily inserted during the process of revision. But one of Emden's points is inadmissible. He comments that "it is inherently unlikely that an author would burlesque two quite different types of novel, the sentimental and the Gothic, at the same time" [409], not realizing that the Gothic novel was really a late development of the sentimental novel, and that the two subforms are often linked together in burlesque works. I would guess that the specifically Gothic extensions of her burlesque occurred to Jane Austen while she was at work on *Northanger Abbey*, and that they were painlessly inserted during the drafting of the first version. Certainly the Gothic sections of the novel support its general themes, and there seems to be no warrant for postulating an early (*c.* 1794) satire on the sentimental novel.

In the *Advertisement* to *Northanger Abbey*, written in 1816, Jane Austen speaks of the novel as "finished in the year 1803, and intended for immediate publication." In the spring of 1803 the manuscript, then called *Susan,* was sold to Crosby and Co. for ten pounds [see the *Life,* pp. 229–33, where the identity of *Susan* and *Northanger Abbey* is established]. But it never appeared, and in 1809 an inquiry revealed that the publisher was willing to return the MS. "for the same as we paid for it" [*Letters,* 5 April 1809]. We know from this inquiry that Jane Austen possessed "another copy" of the novel, and this makes retouching at any time after 1803 a possibility.

After the publication of *Emma* in December 1815 the MS. of *Northanger Abbey* was purchased from the publisher, and its title altered to *Catherine* (possibly, as R. W. Chapman suggests, because a novel called *Susan* had appeared in 1809 [Introductory Note to *Works,* Vol. V]). In 1816 Jane Austen wrote the *Advertisement,* but in March 1817 she informed Fanny Knight that "Miss Catherine is put upon the Shelve for the present, and I do not know that she will ever come out. . . ." [*Letters,* 13 March 1817]. The novel was not published until after her death.

Although R. W. Chapman feels that the change of title from *Susan* to *Catherine* "suggests a more general revision" [*Facts and Problems,* Oxford, 1948, p. 75], there is no reason to believe that *Northanger Abbey* underwent extensive reworking after 1803. Jane Austen's own statement that the novel was "finished" in 1803, combined with the lack of topical references after that date (in her other revisions topical references tend to creep in), leads me to believe that *Northanger Abbey* as a whole is the earliest representative of her mature art. In this I agree with the authors of the *Life,* who say [p. 96] that *Northanger Abbey* offers "the best example of what she could produce at the age of three- or four-and-twenty."

Sense and Sensibility.

Cassandra Austen, in her Memorandum on the composition of her sister's novels, says that *Sense and Sensibility* was begun in November 1797, but that "something of the same story and characters had been written earlier and called Elinor & Marianne" [facsimile, *Minor Works*, facing p. 242]. Of the first version of *Sense and Sensibility* we know nothing beyond the few details given in the *Life* [p. 80]—that it was cast in the epistolary form and written around 1795. The author of the *Memoir* tells us that *Sense and Sensibility* was "begun, in its present form," immediately after the completion of the first version of *Pride and Prejudice (First Impressions)* in November 1797 [p. 49]. But certain details in the final text, such as the references to Scott, point to another revision before publication, and the author of the *Memoir* says elsewhere [p. 101] that the first year of Jane Austen's residence at Chawton (i.e. 1809–10) was "devoted to revising and preparing for the press" *Sense and Sensibility* and *Pride and Prejudice*. The revisions immediately before publication must have been more than cursory; it is hard to believe that Chapter II, for example, was written in 1797–98. Elizabeth Jenkins has suggested that the names "Steele" and "Ferrars" may have been drawn from *La Belle Assemblée* for March 1810 [*Jane Austen*, New York, 1949, p. 64]. But in spite of these evidences of late work one must agree with Miss Jenkins that "not the book's failings only, but, more important, its background and its atmosphere, relate it to the earliest period of her novel-writing."

The Watsons.

The MS. of this fragment is a first draft with revisions, and the watermarks show that it could not have been composed before 1803. It seems probable that the composition did not stretch too far beyond this date; as R. W. Chapman has pointed out, paper was costly and likely to be used soon after purchase [*Facts and Problems*, Oxford, 1948, pp. 49–50]. However, Chapman's argument is not decisive—parts of *Sanditon* (1817) bear an 1812 watermark—and I would lay more emphasis on the failure of Crosby and Co. to publish *Susan*. This failure must have been evident to Jane Austen by the end of 1804, and probably had a great deal to do with her decision to break off work on *The Watsons*. Another disruptive event was the death of her father in January 1805; Fanny Catherine Lefroy, a grand-daughter of James Austen, once stated that "Somewhere in 1804 she [Jane Austen] began 'The Watsons,' but her father died early in 1805, and it was never finished" [*Temple Bar*, LXVII (February 1883), 277].

Pride and Prejudice.

According to Cassandra's Memorandum, *Pride and Prejudice* (then called *First Impressions*) was begun in October 1796 and finished in August 1797. It was later published with "alterations and contractions." On 1 November 1797 Jane Austen's father wrote to Cadell, the publisher, offering for publication at the author's expense "a manuscript novel, comprising 3 volumes, about the length of Miss Burney's *Evelina*," but this offer was declined [*Life*, pp. 96–8]. The final version of *Pride and Prejudice* is actually quite a bit shorter than *Evelina*, pointing to a general revision prior to publication. On 29 January 1813 Jane Austen wrote to Cassandra: "I have lop't and crop't so successfully . . . that I imagine it must be rather shorter than S. & S. altogether." It is impossible to tell whether Jane Austen "lop't and crop't" *First Impressions* or—as R. W. Chapman has suggested [*Works*, II, xiii]—an intermediate 1811 version; but in any case the late revisions were radical ones. R. W. Chapman and Sir Frank MacKinnon have demonstrated that Jane Austen used the calendar of 1811–12 in plotting the novel (see the Appendix to *Works*, Vol. II), and Chapman is surely right when he says that "so intricate a chronological scheme cannot have been patched on to an existing work without extensive revision." Another argument for extensive revision prior to publication is advanced by Miss Lascelles [pp. 30–31]: she points out that Cassandra, who was intimately familiar with *First Impressions*, had not "gone thro' the whole" of *Pride and Prejudice* before publication (see *Letters*, 9 February 1813).

Mansfield Park.

Jane Austen recorded in a fragmentary memorandum on the dates of her own novels [facsimile in *Plan of a Novel,* ed. R. W. Chapman, Oxford, 1926] that *Mansfield Park* was begun "somewhere about Feb^ry 1811" and finished "soon after June 1813." Jane Austen may have done some preliminary work on the novel before 1811, but there is no reason to accept Dr. Chapman's hypothesis (in an Appendix to *Works,* Vol. III) that the novel is based on the almanacs of 1808–09. As I have demonstrated elsewhere [*Notes & Queries,* CCVI (June 1961), 221–2.] the calendars for 1796–97 are even more appropriate, since the date of Easter 1797 (16 April) coincides exactly with the date indicated in the novel. It is possible that Jane Austen began her major work on *Mansfield Park* with notes or a rough fragment carried over from the first half of her artistic career.

Emma.

According to Jane Austen's own Memorandum, *Emma* was begun on 21 January 1814 and completed on 29 March 1815.

Persuasion.

The novel was begun on 8 August 1815 and finished on 6 August 1816 (Jane Austen's Memorandum). The MS. of the canceled Chap. X and the original Chap. XI (now XII) bears the date "*Finis. July 18. 1816.*"—presumably the period from July 18th to August 6th was devoted to the rewriting of Chap. X. Although in a letter of 13 March 1817 Jane Austen speaks of *Persuasion* as ready for publication, we may assume that the entire MS. would have undergone a general retouching if she had lived. It seems to have been Jane Austen's habit to allow a MS. to rest for some time before undertaking the final revision.

Sanditon.

This fragment was written between 27 January and 17 March 1817 [*Life*, pp. 381–2]. Presumably it was broken off because of failing health.

NOTES

Chapter I

1. Ian Watt elaborates upon this point in *The Rise of the Novel*, London, 1960, pp. 296–7. Watt's study is the best general survey of the major eighteenth-century English novelists and their social-philosophic background.

2. Johnson's most important comments on the influence of the novel are found in *Rambler* No. 4 (1750). For a survey of late eighteenth-century criticism of fiction, see Joseph B. Heidler, *The History, from 1700 to 1800, of English Criticism of Prose Fiction*, University of Illinois Studies in Language and Literature, XIII (May 1928). The most extensive history of prose fiction written before 1790, Clara Reeve's *Progress of Romance* (1785), perpetuates Dr. Johnson's conviction that the novel, because of its plausible action, is potentially a greater threat to morality than the romance.

3. Scott's notice appeared in the *Quarterly Review*, XIV (October 1815), 188–201. One of the important impulses toward more serious criticism of fiction came with the establishment of the *Edinburgh Review* and the *Quarterly*.

4. Comic reactions to popular fiction, while rare before 1790, flourished in the last decade of the century. See A. B. Shepperson, *The Novel in Motley*, Cambridge, Mass., 1936, especially Chap.

V; and Winfield H. Rogers, "The Reaction Against Melodramatic Sentimentality in the English Novel, 1796–1830," *PMLA*, XLIX (March 1934), 98–122.

5. The best survey of Jane Austen's reading is the chapter on "Reading and Response" in Mary Lascelles, *Jane Austen and Her Art*, London, 1939, pp. 41–83.

6. F. R. Leavis, *The Great Tradition*, London, 1948, p. 5.

7. These figures are based on Appendix E in Frank G. Black's *The Epistolary Novel in the Late Eighteenth Century*, Eugene, Ore., 1940. For an assessment of changes in the eighteenth-century reading public see Ian Watt, *Rise of the Novel*, Chap. II; I am indebted to Watt for the general argument of this paragraph.

8. *The Rivals*, I, ii.

9. *The Borough*, Letter XX ("Ellen Orford"); *Quarterly Review*, XIV (October 1815), 190.

10. "Jane Austen," *North British Review*, LII [N.S., XIII] (April-July 1870), 130. The author of this article has been identified as Richard Simpson, the Shakespearean scholar (see *Jane Austen: A Collection of Critical Essays*, ed. Ian Watt, Englewood Cliffs, N.J., 1963, pp. 5, 14n.).

11. This is roughly the distinction used by E. A. Baker in his *History of the English Novel*, Vol. V.

12. *The School for Widows*, London, 1791, Vol. I, p. vi.

13. The editor was Henry Morley, in an edition of 1886; quoted in Hamish Miles's edition of the novel, London, 1928, p. 28.

14. *The Fool of Quality*, ed. E. A. Baker, London, 1906, p. 392 (Chap. XVIII).

15. Ibid. p. 319 (Chap. XVII).

16. Quoted in Lascelles, p. 54.

17. *Diary of Fanny Burney*, 8 June 1780 (Everyman edition, pp. 50–51).

18. Mudrick, p. 36.

19. *Rambler* No. 4.

20. *The Loiterer*, No. 47, Oxford, 1789. This periodical, which was edited by Jane Austen's older brother James, is discussed on pp. 15–17 of the present study.

21. This is the leading argument of Mudrick's *Jane Austen: Irony as Defense and Discovery*.

22. The formula was popular for well over fifty years; we might take as chronological limits Charlotte Lennox's *Female Quixote*

(1752) and Eaton Stannard Barrett's *The Heroine* (1813). Jane Austen was familiar with both these works (see *Letters*, 7 January 1807 and 2 March 1814; the first of these letters indicates that Jane Austen knew the *Female Quixote* when she was a young girl).

23. The unfinished burlesque was not published until 1839. See Shepperson, pp. 92–5.

24. For the theatricals at Steventon see *Life*, pp. 63–6. The allusion to *The Critic* in *The History of England* may be found on p. 148 of the *Minor Works*; see pp. 19–23 of this study for a discussion of the parody in *Love and Freindship*.

25. For a full discussion of the periodical and its relationship to Jane Austen's art, see my article "*The Loiterer*: A Reflection of Jane Austen's Early Environment," *Review of English Studies*, N.S., XII (August 1961), 251–61.

26. *Life*, p. 48, and *Memoir*, p. 12.

27. *Life*, p. 57. This "second stage" followed soon after the publication of *The Loiterer*.

28. Mary Lascelles, "Miss Austen and Some Books," *The London Mercury*, XXIX (April 1934), 530.

29. C. L. Thomson, *Jane Austen*, London, 1929, p. 60.

30. *The Critic*, III, i. B. C. Southam has noted this allusion in his edition of *Volume the Second* (p. 211).

31. See footnote 4 above.

32. Mudrick, p. 10. Mudrick makes a good case (pp. 5–12) for *Laura and Augustus* as a major source of *Love and Freindship*. In his *History of the Pre-Romantic Novel in England*, New York, 1949, p. 199, James R. Foster remarks that *Laura and Augustus* was "doubtless the novel, or at least one of the novels, Jane Austen had in mind when she wrote *Love and Freindship* . . ."

33. See Annette B. Hopkins, "Jane Austen's 'Love and Freindship': A Study in Literary Relations," *The South Atlantic Quarterly*, XXIV (January 1925), 48, where the claim is made that if *The Watsons* is included with the early works "there is not a single one of the six mature novels whose beginnings, if only minutely, cannot be detected here, in a genre, a situation, a character, or a mere name."

34. *Letters*, 9 September 1814.

35. The MS. of *Love and Freindship* is dated 13 June 1790; the letters in "Lesley Castle" are dated January-April 1792.

36. Mudrick, p. 27.
37. See footnote 53.
38. Black, op. cit. p. 104.
39. There is evidence that Jane Austen was still retouching *Volume the Third* in 1809, or at least still interested in its stories. One letter in *Evelyn* (190) is dated "Aug^st 19th 1809," and in *Catharine* Jane Austen replaced a reference to Bishop Secker's explanation of the Catechism by one to Hannah More's *Coelebs,* first published in 1809. This return to *Volume the Third* was probably part of a general revival of interest in her art.
40. Mudrick, p. 20.
41. Brooke, *The Fool of Quality,* p. 251 (Chap. XVI).
42. See Chap. II, pp. 67–8.
43. See A. R. Humphreys, " 'The Friend of Mankind' (1700–60)— An Aspect of Eighteenth-Century Sensibility," *Review of English Studies,* XXIV (July 1948), 218. It is interesting to note that the "amiable Maria" shines in "that favourite character of Sir Charles Grandison's, a nurse" (186).
44. On 8 July 1774 Wesley wrote to Henry Brooke, Jr.: "I could not but observe the design of it *[The Fool of Quality],* to promote the religion of the heart. . . ." [E. A. Baker, Introduction to *The Fool of Quality,* p. xxvii]. Wesley's abridged edition was published in 1781 under the title *The History of Henry, Earl of Moreland.*
45. David Paul, "The Gay Apprentice," *The Twentieth Century,* CLVI (December 1954), 547.
46. Reginald Farrer, "Jane Austen," *Quarterly Review,* CCXXVIII (July 1917), 15.
47. Mudrick, p. 127.
48. Ibid. p. 140.
49. *The Watsons,* on the evidence of the watermarks, could not have been written before 1803 (the MS. is a corrected draft, not a fair copy as with *Lady Susan*).
50. *Life,* p. 80.
51. Ibid.
52. Lascelles, pp. 13–14.
53. For Jane Austen's relationship with Eliza de Feuillide, see pp. 117–21 of the present study. In Chap. VI of M. A. Austen-Leigh's *Personal Aspects of Jane Austen,* London, 1920, the author argues

for an early dating of *Lady Susan,* and claims that Jane Austen based her fiction on an anecdote known to the family.

54. See Jay Arnold Levine, "*Lady Susan:* Jane Austen's Character of the Merry Widow," *Studies in English Literature* (Rice University), I (Autumn 1961), 23–34, for an analysis of *Lady Susan* that emphasizes Jane Austen's dependence on literary models. Levine shares the view that *Lady Susan* should be grouped with the mature *Juvenilia.*

55. Mudrick, p. 138.

56. Ibid. p. 139.

57. *Letters,* 28 September 1814.

58. Lascelles, p. 107.

59. Howard S. Babb's recent study, *Jane Austen's Novels: The Fabric of Dialogue,* Columbus, 1962, is an illuminating analysis of the relation between dialogue and dramatic action in Jane Austen's major works. Of especial interest are his comments on general terms and figurative language in Chapter I.

60. *Letters,* 14 September 1804.

61. In his Appendix on "Miss Austen's English" in *Works,* Vol. I.

62. From "Jack & Alice" in *Volume the First* (VI, 13).

63. For the connection between Johnson's "moral purpose" and his "bent for generality" see W. K. Wimsatt, *The Prose Style of Samuel Johnson,* New Haven, 1941, especially p. 55.

64. *Letters,* 9 September 1814.

65. For these examples see *Minor Works,* pp. 11, 37, 79.

66. Evidence for the popularity of the epistolary novel may be found in Appendix E of Black's *The Epistolary Novel. . . .*

67. From the essay on Mackenzie in *Lives of the Novelists.*

68. "Preface by the Editor" to *Pamela.*

69. See the author's Preface to *Camilla.*

70. Thomson, *Jane Austen,* p. 45.

71. *Letters,* 18 December 1798.

72. Review of *Northanger Abbey* and *Persuasion* in the *Quarterly Review,* XXIV (January 1821), 352–76.

73. It is a sign of our new attitude toward Jane Austen's fiction that a number of recent critics have pointed out the similarities between her technical aims and those of James. For a rather thin survey of these similarities see I. Simon, "Jane Austen and *The Art of the Novel,*" *English Studies,* XLIII (August 1962), 225–39.

CHAPTER II

1. For a discussion of the problems involved in dating this novel and Jane Austen's other works, see the Appendix on Chronology of Composition.
2. See the Chronological Appendix and C. S. Emden, "*Northanger Abbey* Re-Dated?," *Notes and Queries*, CXCV (16 September 1950), 407–10.
3. For a discussion of some of these burlesques see A. B. Shepperson, *The Novel in Motley*, Cambridge, Mass., 1936, Chap. VIII.
4. In the *Advertisement* to *Northanger Abbey*.
5. *Magasin encyclopédique*, 3ᵉ année, t. IV (1797), 133. Translation from D. P. Varma, *The Gothic Flame*, London, 1957, pp. 179–80.
6. Mary Lascelles, "Miss Austen and Some Books," *The London Mercury*, XXIX (April 1934), 528–9, and C. L. Thomson, *Jane Austen*, London, 1929, pp. 124–33.
7. Michael Sadleir, *The Northanger Novels*, The English Association Pamphlets, No. 68, November 1927.
8. *Letters*, 2 March 1814.
9. From the essay on Mrs. Radcliffe in *Lives of the Novelists*.
10. Lionel Trilling, "*Mansfield Park*," in *The Opposing Self*, New York, 1955, p. 207. For an exaggerated treatment of this theme see John K. Mathison, "*Northanger Abbey* and Jane Austen's Conception of the Value of Fiction," *Journal of English Literary History*, XXIV (June 1957), 138–52.
11. In a footnote to his "Introductory Note to *Northanger Abbey* and *Persuasion*" (p. xiii, fn. 2) R. W. Chapman points out that "Henry's reference to St. George's Fields makes it certain that he is thinking of the Gordon Riots of 1780."
12. D. W. Harding, "Regulated Hatred: An Aspect of the Work of Jane Austen," *Scrutiny*, VIII (March 1940), 347–8.
13. James to A. C. Benson in 1896. See F. W. Dupee, *Henry James*, New York, 1951, p. 220.
14. Kenneth Clark, *The Gothic Revival*, Revised edn., London, 1950, pp. 62–3.
15. See Lascelles, pp. 157–8, and Ian Jack, "The Epistolary Element in Jane Austen," *English Studies Today, Second Series*, ed. G. A. Bonnard, Bern, 1961, pp. 173–86.

16. For discussion of this problem see J. M. S. Tompkins, *"Elinor and Marianne:* A Note on Jane Austen," *Review of English Studies,* XVI (January 1940), 33–43, and Martin Melander, "An Unknown Source of Jane Austen's *Sense and Sensibility," Studia Neophilologica,* XXII (1950), 146–70. Although there are a few striking similarities between *A Gossip's Story* and *Sense and Sensibility* which suggest that Jane Austen may have borrowed some details from it, the date of publication (1796) and the wide disparities in attitude make it difficult to accept the opinion that *A Gossip's Story* was the "starting-point" for *Elinor and Marianne.*

17. The *Letters of Julia and Caroline* appeared in *Letters for Literary Ladies,* London, 1795. This was the first of Maria Edgeworth's published works.

18. Ibid. p. 3.

19. Ibid. pp. 4–6.

20. Ibid. p. 7.

21. Ibid. p. 26.

22. The distinction between "natural" and "excessive" sensibility was a commonplace. The author of the article on "Sensibility" in the Third Edition of the *Encyclopaedia Britannica* (1797) contends that sensibility, "as far as it is natural, seems to depend upon the organization of the nervous system." All the qualities of sensibility that are not born in man "may be resolved into association," and are to be "regulated accordingly." He goes on:

> It is . . . a matter of some moment to distinguish real sensibilities from ridiculous affections; those which tend to increase the sum of human happiness from such as have a contrary tendency, and to cultivate them all in such a manner as to make them answer the ends for which they were implanted in us by the beneficent Author of nature. This can be done only by watching over them as over other associations . . . for excessive sensibility, as it is not the gift of nature, is the bane of human happiness.

23. For an excellent discussion of the language of *Sense and Sensibility* see Howard S. Babb, *Jane Austen's Novels: The Fabric of Dialogue,* Columbus, 1962, Chapter III. Babb's analyses of the novel's dialogue reinforce the argument of this chapter.

24. Frank O'Connor, "Jane Austen: The Flight from Fancy," in *The Mirror in the Roadway,* London, 1957, p. 25.

25. Mudrick, pp. 90–93.

CHAPTER III

1. The title *"The Watsons"* was given to the MS. by the author of the *Memoir,* James Edward Austen-Leigh. The MS., if not a first draft, is a very early version, displaying numerous corrections and alterations. Some sheets bear the watermark "1803." For a description of the MS. and a complete record of the revisions see R. W. Chapman's separate edition, Oxford University Press, 1927. In Vol. VI of the *Works* Chapman prints only Jane Austen's "final intention."

    For details of the history of *Susan* see R. W. Chapman's Preface to *Works,* Vol. V.

2. According to the author of the *Memoir,* Cassandra told her nieces "something of the intended story." "Mr. Watson was soon to die; and Emma to become dependent for a home on her narrow-minded sister-in-law and brother. She was to decline an offer of marriage from Lord Osborne, and much of the interest of the tale was to arise from Lady [i.e. Miss] Osborne's love for Mr. Howard, and his counter-affection for Emma, whom he was finally to marry" [see *Works,* Vol. VI, pp. 362–3]. There seems to be no merit in the *Memoir*'s suggestion that Jane Austen abandoned *The Watsons* because she became aware "of the evil of having placed her heroine too low, in a position of poverty and obscurity" [see R. W. Chapman, *Jane Austen: Facts and Problems,* Oxford, 1948, pp. 50–51].

3. Mudrick, pp. 141–5.

4. Lascelles, pp. 99–100.

5. Mudrick, p. 153.

6. The similarities between *The Watsons* and *Emma* have been noted by many critics. R. W. Chapman points out [*Facts and Problems,* p. 51] the basic parallels: both stories take place in Surrey, Mr. Watson reminds one of Mr. Woodhouse, Mrs. Robert Watson is "strikingly suggestive" of Mrs. Elton, Emma Watson's situation is like that of Jane Fairfax, the characters of the two Emmas are "not unlike." But these parallels do not justify Mrs. Leavis's opinion that *The Watsons* was rewritten as *Emma* [Q. D. Leavis, "A Critical Theory of Jane Austen's Writings," *Scrutiny,* X (June 1941), 76–84]. Jane Austen was simply ex-

ploring in *The Watsons* the world of *Mansfield Park, Emma,* and *Persuasion.*

7. *Letters,* 10 August 1814.
8. Ibid.
9. Lionel Trilling, *The Liberal Imagination,* New York, 1950, pp. 206–7.
10. *Letters,* 29 January 1813.
11. See the *Letters,* Nos. 95 (May or June 1814), 98 (10 August 1814), 100 (9 September 1814), and 101 (28 September 1814).
12. Lascelles, p. 99.
13. 1927 O.U.P. edition, pp. 4 and 11; *Works,* Vol. VI, pp. 316 and 319. In subsequent footnotes the page number of the separate edition will be followed by the page reference to *Works,* Vol. VI, in brackets.
14. 107 [357].
15. 19, 20 [322].
16. *Letters,* 9 September 1814.
17. See the chronological appendices to the novels in Chapman's edition, and Sir Frank MacKinnon's "Topography and Travel in Jane Austen's Novels," in *The Murder in the Temple and Other Holiday Tasks,* London, 1935, pp. 86–109.
18. R. W. Chapman, "Jane Austen's Methods," *Times Literary Supplement,* 9 February 1922.
19. 107 [357].
20. 45 [332].
21. 57 [337].
22. 110–12 [358–9].
23. 79–80 [346].
24. The words "It was a new thing with him to wish to please a woman; it was the first time that he had ever felt" are written over the erased fragment "You have not been long in this Country I understand.—I hope you are pleased with its—the delicate."
25. *Letters,* 9 February 1813.
26. Lascelles, p. 31.
27. See the Appendix on the Chronology of *Pride and Prejudice* in *Works,* Vol. II.
28. Mary Lascelles remarks [p. 30] that *Sense and Sensibility* "was never to account for as much, to the author or her family, as the later novels: she would—'if asked'—tell them what became of

Miss Steele, but her own imagination did not linger in the world of *Sense and Sensibility* as it was to do in that of *Pride and Prejudice.*"

29. *Letters,* 24 May 1813.

30. *Letters,* 29 January 1813.

31. *Works,* Vol. V. p. 4.

32. For discussion of the relationship between Fanny Burney and Jane Austen, and between *Cecilia* and *Pride and Prejudice,* see C. L. Thomson, *Jane Austen,* London, 1929, p. 100–106; Elizabeth Jenkins, *Jane Austen,* New York, 1949, pp. 49–57; Q. D. Leavis, "A Critical Theory of Jane Austen's Writings," *Scrutiny,* X (June 1941), 71–2; and R. W. Chapman's Appendix to *Works,* Vol. II. *Evelina* (1778) and *Cecilia* (1782) were well known to Jane Austen before she began *First Impressions* (1796), and *Camilla* was published in that year (with Jane Austen as one of the subscribers).

33. Leavis, op. cit. p. 71.

34. Jenkins, op. cit. p. 51.

35. Lionel Trilling, *The Opposing Self,* New York, 1955, p. 222.

36. Shaftesbury gave currency to the notion that the moral sense and the aesthetic sense spring from the same faculties. See William E. Alderman, "Shaftesbury and the Doctrine of Moral Sense in the Eighteenth Century," *PMLA,* XLVI (December 1931), 1087–94.

37. Scott's review of *Emma* in the *Quarterly Review,* XIV (October 1815), 194.

38. Mark Schorer, "Pride Unprejudiced," *Kenyon Review,* XVIII (Winter 1956), 72–91.

39. See Howard S. Babb, *Jane Austen's Novels: The Fabric of Dialogue,* Columbus, 1962, pp. 113–42; Reuben A. Brower, "Light and Bright and Sparkling: Irony and Fiction in *Pride and Prejudice,*" in *The Fields of Light,* New York, 1951, pp. 164–81; R. J. Schoeck, "Jane Austen and the Sense of Exposure: Heuristics in *Pride and Prejudice,*" *English Studies,* XXXVI (August 1955), 154–7; and Dorothy Van Ghent, *The English Novel: Form and Function,* New York, 1953, pp. 99–111.

40. Brower, op. cit. especially pp. 164–5.

41. *Letters,* 29 January 1813.

42. Babb, op. cit. pp. 132–41.

Chapter IV

1. Facsimile in *Works*, Vol. VI (facing page 242).
2. Lionel Trilling, *"Mansfield Park,"* in *The Opposing Self*, New York, 1955, p. 211.
3. Typical of these critics is Reginald Farrer, who finds the novel "vitiated throughout by a radical dishonesty, that was certainly not in its author's own nature" ["Jane Austen," *Quarterly Review*, CCXXVIII (July 1917), 20].
4. See my comments on the dating of *Mansfield Park* in the Chronological Appendix.
5. In 1809 Jane Austen declared, in a letter to Cassandra, "I do not like the Evangelicals." But five years later, when advising her niece Fanny on the choice of a suitor, she said: "And as to there being any objection from his *Goodness*, from the danger of his becoming even Evangelical, I cannot admit *that*. I am by no means convinced that we ought not all to be Evangelicals, & am at least persuaded that they who are so from Reason and Feeling, must be happiest & safest. . . . Wisdom is better than Wit, & in the long run will certainly have the laugh on her side . . ." [*Letters*, 24 January 1809 and 18 November 1814]. This would seem to imply a real change in attitude coincident with the writing of *Mansfield Park*, although it is clear that Jane Austen never cared for the dramatization of religious feelings (see her letter to Cassandra of 8 September 1816). We should remember that Henry Austen, Jane's favorite brother, ultimately became "an earnest preacher of the evangelical school" [*Life*, p. 333].
6. *Letters*, 29 January 1813.
7. *Letters*, 18 November 1814.
8. Trilling, op. cit. p. 218.
9. For details of the relationship between Eliza and the Austen family, see *Life*, pp. 34–45; Elizabeth Jenkins, *Jane Austen*, New York, 1949, pp. 20–24; and the *Austen Papers*, ed. R. A. Austen-Leigh, London, 1942, Chaps. V and VI. One of those who accepts the identification of Eliza and Mary Crawford without qualification is Q. D. Leavis, "A Critical Theory of Jane Austen's Writings (II): 'Lady Susan' into 'Mansfield Park,'" *Scrutiny*, X (October 1941), 141.

10. R. W. Chapman, *Jane Austen: Facts and Problems*, Oxford, 1948, pp. 127–9.

11. *Austen Papers*, pp. 123–6.

12. Ibid. p. 128.

13. Ibid.

14. See John H. Hubback, "Pen Portraits in Jane Austen's Novels," *The Cornhill Magazine*, LXV (July 1928), 27–8.

15. *Austen Papers*, p. 160 (Eliza to Philadelphia, 3 May 1797).

16. Ibid. p. 131 (Phila to James Walter, 23 July 1788).

17. Trilling, op. cit. p. 219.

18. R. W. Chapman, Note to the text of *Lovers' Vows* published as an appendix in *Works*, Vol. III. There may have been many more than four adaptations; in the Preface to her "exact" English version (Dublin, 1798) Ann Plumptre claims that the play was pirated twelve times before official publication.

19. For information on the adaptations and performances of *Lovers' Vows* see L. F. Thompson, *Kotzebue: A Survey of His Progress in France and England*, Paris, 1928, especially p. 63.

20. William Reitzel, "*Mansfield Park* and *Lovers' Vows*," *Review of English Studies*, IX (October 1933), 454n.

21. E. M. Butler, "*Mansfield Park* and Kotzebue's *Lovers' Vows*," *Modern Language Review*, XXVIII (July 1933), 326–37. Miss Butler claims that *Mansfield Park* "is nothing more or less than *Lovers' Vows* translated into real life with the moral standard subverted by Kotzebue neatly re-inverted." She attempts to document a detailed correspondence between the two plots, but in so doing she distorts the events of both the play and the novel, and is forced to equate several characters in *Mansfield Park* with each character in *Lovers' Vows*. See the reply to Miss Butler by H. Winifred Husbands, *MLR*, XXIX (April 1934), 176–9.

22. *Biographia Literaria*, ed. J. Shawcross, Oxford, 1907, II, 159. Coleridge is referring to "the weeping comedies of Kotzebue and his imitators."

23. Reitzel, op. cit. p. 453.

24. Trilling, op. cit. p. 218.

25. For an interesting but rather schematic application of the Cinderella story to *Mansfield Park*, see David Paul, "The Gay Apprentice," *The Twentieth Century*, CLVI (December 1954), 549–50.

Chapter V

1. *Letters*, 11 December 1815.
2. *Letters*, 4 February 1813.
3. *Memoir*, p. 157.
4. In recent years several critics have produced excellent studies of the relation between Emma's development and the novel's narrative structure. See Joseph M. Duffy, Jr., "*Emma*: The Awakening from Innocence," *ELH*, XXI (March 1954), 39–53; Edgar F. Shannon, "*Emma*: Character and Construction," *PMLA*, LXXI (September 1956), 637–50; Lionel Trilling, "*Emma*," *Encounter*, VIII (June 1957), 49–59; and Wayne C. Booth, "Point of View and the Control of Distance in *Emma*," *Nineteenth Century Fiction*, XVI (September 1961), 95–116 (later reprinted in Booth's *The Rhetoric of Fiction*, Chicago, 1961).
5. "*De Descriptione Temporum*, An Inaugural Lecture," in *They Asked for a Paper*, London, 1962, p. 17.
6. In his essay on *Emma* Lionel Trilling remarks that, "like Don Quixote and Emma Bovary, her mind [Emma's] is shaped and deceived by fiction . . ." [*Encounter*, VIII (June 1957), 55].
7. *Rasselas*, Chap. XXXII.
8. Quoted in Alan McKillop, *Samuel Richardson: Printer and Novelist*, Chapel Hill, 1936, p. 127.
9. Henry James, *The Art of Fiction and Other Essays*, New York, 1948, p. 13.
10. See the Prefaces to *The Ambassadors* and *The Wings of the Dove*.
11. *Letters*, 9 September 1814.
12. Wayne C. Booth, *The Rhetoric of Fiction*, Chicago, 1961, pp. 256–8.

Chapter VI

1. Kenneth Clark, *Landscape Into Art*, London, 1949, Chap. III.
2. From the Biographical Notice, *Works*, Vol. V, p. 7.
3. Jane Austen's use of the seasons in *Emma* is analyzed by Edgar Shannon in "*Emma*: Character and Construction," *PMLA*, LXXI (September 1956), 647–8.

4. E. M. Forster, *Abinger Harvest*, London, 1936, p. 150.

5. D. H. Lawrence, *Apropos of Lady Chatterley's Lover*, London, 1930, pp. 57–8.

6. Wayne C. Booth, *The Rhetoric of Fiction*, Chicago, 1961, p. 251.

7. *Two Chapters of "Persuasion*," Oxford, 1926.

8. Ibid. p. 13.

9. Ibid. p. 16.

10. Lascelles, p. 39. *Sanditon* actually contains twelve chapters.

11. All but one of the quotations from *Sanditon* used in this chapter are taken from the *Minor Works*, where R. W. Chapman records what seems to have been Jane Austen's final intention.

12. *Letters*, 2 March 1814.

13. Constance Hill, *Jane Austen: Her Homes & Her Friends*, London, 1904, p. 195.

14. Ibid. See also *Letters*, annotation to No. 102.

15. *Letters*, No. 102 (Summer 1814).

16. *Letters*, No. 113a (J. S. Clarke to Jane Austen, 16 November 1815).

17. *Letters*, 11 December 1815.

18. *Plan of a Novel* is reprinted in *Minor Works*. For the surrounding documents, including the correspondence between Mr. Clarke and Jane Austen, see the separate edition of the *Plan* (ed. R. W. Chapman, Oxford, 1926).

19. *Minor Works*, pp. 428, 430.

20. *Fragment of a Novel*, ed. R. W. Chapman, Oxford, 1925.

21. *Letters*, 9 September 1814.

22. E. M. Forster, *Abinger Harvest*, p. 151.

23. *Fragment of a Novel*, pp. 51–2. In the first sentence I have followed B. C. Southam's reading of "real" for Chapman's "neat" [B. C. Southam, "The Text of 'Sanditon,'" *Notes and Queries*, CCVI (January 1961), 23–4].

24. R. W. Chapman, *Jane Austen: Facts and Problems*, Oxford, 1948, p. 209.

INDEX

195